The Language of Cosmetics Advertising

Helen Ringrow

The Language of Cosmetics Advertising

palgrave
macmillan

Helen Ringrow
School of Languages and Area Studies
University of Portsmouth
Portsmouth, United Kingdom

ISBN 978-1-137-55797-1   ISBN 978-1-137-55798-8   (eBook)
DOI 10.1057/978-1-137-55798-8

Library of Congress Control Number: 2016947438

Printed on acid-free paper

This Palgrave Pivot imprint is published by Springer Nature
The registered company is Macmillan publishers Ltd. London

For Olivia and Leah

ACKNOWLEDGEMENTS

I would like to thank all of my supportive colleagues at the University of Portsmouth, Queen's University Belfast, and beyond. It seems clichéd to state there are too many to mention, but it is true. My sincere thanks in particular go to Paul Simpson, Janice Carruthers, Andrea Mayr, Simon Statham, Manuel Jobert, Clara Neary, Ben Clarke, Thomas Rodgers, Alessia Tranchese, James Bullock, Mario Saraceni, Sue Wright, Emily Horrocks, and Caoimhe Nic Lochlainn. Funding from the Department for Employment and Learning (NI) and the Centre for European and International Studies Research (Portsmouth) made this project possible. Thanks to the Société de Stylistique Anglaise for the reproduction of material in Chapter 5. I am also grateful to Palgrave Macmillan for their support during the publishing process.

Thank you to my family and friends on both sides of the Irish Sea, especially to my mum, Anne. Thanks to Adam for fixing a lot of problems, technical and otherwise, and thanks to Louise for proofreading.

Last but definitely not least, thank you to Niall for all the moral support.

CONTENTS

LIST OF FIGURES

LIST OF TABLES

CHAPTER 1

Beauty Advertising in a Cross-Cultural Context

Abstract This chapter outlines some key current debates around gender, media, and identity. It argues that beauty advertisements merit attention from the perspective of critical linguistics in order to interrogate gender ideals in contemporary media discourse. This chapter also explains the data used throughout the book and the overall approach taken, which is that of Feminist Critical Discourse Analysis.

Keywords Gender and media • Gender and identity • Cosmetics advertisements • Advertising across cultures • Feminist Critical Discourse Analysis

GENDER, MEDIA, AND IDENTITY

This book explores how a certain kind of 'femininity' is constructed through the language of cosmetics advertising. The relationship between gender, the mass media, and identity is often complex. In much contemporary Western[1] media, there exists a strong connection between femininity and an attractive appearance, which can be found in both language and images depicting and/or targeting women. From Disney princesses to reality television makeover shows, female appearance from childhood through to adulthood tends to be foregrounded in a way that male appearance is not.

This 'double standard' generally manifests itself in an increased media focus on female looks above success: Hillary Clinton's cleavage, Sarah Palin's beehive, and Michelle Obama's upper arms being just three examples in a recent US political context (Rhode 2010: 10). As Greer laments: 'every woman knows that, regardless of all her other achievements, she is a failure if she is not beautiful' (2007: 23). Although women's actual thoughts, behaviour, and purchasing patterns are on many occasions far removed from their discursive media representations, the predominant mainstream constructions of femininity are worthy of careful examination and critique in order to dissect their underlying ideologies (Gill 2007: 217). In this context, cosmetics advertising texts are often best conceptualised as sites of struggle where the actual reader may be 'hailed' into a certain subject position which they can accept, reject, or otherwise respond (Althusser 1969; see also Mills 2012: 44).

The majority of cosmetics are marketed using the message that the female appearance can be improved with the aid of products: one has the opportunity to look younger, slimmer, prettier, and so on. Although progress has been made with regard to gender equality in several arenas of society, sexist media representations still prevail and women's bodies tend to be viewed as commodities to look at whilst simultaneously constructed as sites for improvement (Byerly and Ross 2006: 37–38). The female body is often presented as always needing 'work' in order to conform to the 'ever narrower judgements of female attractiveness' (Gill 2007: 255). The 'fat' female body is increasingly seen as problematic in this contemporary media discourse, signalling a lack of control within the context of medical narratives about obesity (Murray 2008). The presupposition in media discourse is that women *want* to improve their appearance, and that they will do so through particular cosmetics (Gill 2007: 135). This is not to say that women cannot or should not modify their looks; rather, the issue lies with the pervasiveness and restrictiveness of these media constructs. Women who do *not* want to change their appearance through beauty products and other 'feminising' practices may be positioned as outside of the norm portrayed in the media. Many women enjoy such activities,[2] but often the emphasis on 'playfulness' and 'fun' can disguise the fact that these practices are routinely expected and prescribed, and opting out may be difficult or even seemingly impossible for some women (Gill 2007: 182). There exists a tension in the feminist scholarship between the potential harm caused by regarding cosmetics as necessary items to 'fix' the female appearance versus the (somewhat contested) potential pleasure gained by their usage (Smith 1988; Wolf 1991; Walter 1999: 87–103; Hollows 2000: 157; Gauntlett 2008: 85–87; Talbot 2010: 38; Jones 2010: 365; Rhode 2010: 88). The position adopted in this book is that cosmetics advertising should be examined and critiqued in order to challenge the taken-for-granted assumptions that are often found there: heteronormativity, stereotypical 'feminine' and 'masculine' identities, and an overarching emphasis on physical beauty, amongst many others. This process may enable us as consumers to become more critically engaged with the ever-pervasive domain of cosmetics advertising. In this vein, critical linguistic analysis gives us the tools to unpack product claims; to identify presuppositions that may reinforce outdated gendered stereotypes; and to consider how consumers may challenge the ways in which they are addressed through cosmetic advertising discourse. Critical discourse research can be a first step in the process of societal change and should aim to both question and reform existing discourses (Toolan 1997).

Cosmetics advertising should be situated within the context of the global beauty business, which has been enjoying unprecedented growth worldwide. Advertising and marketing campaigns are key ways of penetrating new markets, creating brand awareness, maximising product sales, and, ideally, achieving customer loyalty. In 2008, consumers worldwide spent $330 billion on fragrances, cosmetics, and toiletries (Jones 2010: 1); and research by Mint in 2013 suggests that this figure has increased to $382 billion from an estimated 85 % female base.[3] Globalisation, whether viewed productively in terms of market freedom or as contributing to gross inequalities (or somewhere between these two viewpoints),[4] has not created uniform convergence of worldwide consumers with exactly the same needs, wants, and desires (de Mooij 2010: 2). Many cosmetics products are sold in different cultural and linguistic contexts, and there may be slight changes in terms of the adaptation-localisation ratio in order to effectively appeal to the target demographic (Kelly-Holmes 2005: 7; Machin and van Leeuwen 2007: 105; see also Munday 2004; Sidiropoulou 2008; Woodward-Smith and Eynullaeva 2009). With regard to the English and French contexts in which this current research is situated, there is much overlap in the type of cosmetic being sold (and indeed sometimes they are exactly the same). One difference is the increased advertising and consumption of 'slimming creams' in France, which do not as yet have the same market share in the United Kingdom (these creams are explored in particular in Chapter 5 of this book).

Cosmetics advertisements in Britain and Metropolitan France are subject to regulation in terms of what they can or cannot claim about a product. L'Autorité de Régulation Professionnelle de la Publicité (L'ARPP) is the French independent body regulating advertising, approximately equivalent to the UK's Advertising Standards Authority (ASA).[5] Both organisations advise companies and advertising agencies on how to best comply with their codes of practice, in addition to responding to consumer queries and complaints. In some cases, they may recommend advertisements change their content and can withdraw adverts due to non-compliance. However, even if advertisements *do* follow the guidelines, the language used could still be potentially misleading and/or affirm certain ideological positions. The ASA emphasises that cosmetics advertising is often aspirational, in that people may be encouraged to look better, but these claims should be founded in reality. Both the ASA and the ARPP advise that any claims made must be supported with appropriate scientific evidence, and a beauty product's effectiveness should not be exaggerated.[6] The two regulatory bodies make a distinction between temporary and permanent effects on the skin, in addition to changes to the skin itself and changes simply to the skin's appearance. For example, hair is not necessarily healthier, but may *look* healthier for a short time after use of a certain shampoo. In practice, claims of temporary benefits are generally issue-free from a regulatory standpoint, but permanent physiological changes require appropriate clinical evidence for support. The ASA gives further advice with regard to specific vocabulary items. For skin products, acceptable lexis includes 'reduce the appearance of fine lines and wrinkles'; 'plump'; 'temporarily lift and firm skin'; and 'younger looking skin'. Unacceptable lexis includes 'permanently reduce fine lines and wrinkles'; 'permanently lift or firm skin'; 'sculpt the body'; 'reduce cellulite'; and references to Botox.[7]

Images in cosmetic advertisements are also subject to regulation. The issue of airbrushing has recently attracted much attention in the UK press, and the ASA has been known to withdraw high-profile advertisements where the post-production techniques may have given a misleading impression of product performance. Pre- and post-production visual editing techniques are widespread and generally acceptable provided the consumer is not misled about what can be achieved through product usage. As such, advertisers are now required to show 'before' and 'after' shots of visual editing on request.[8]

Discursive Constructions of Femininity in English and French Cosmetics Advertisements

The overall aim of this book is to explore how femininity is discursively constructed in contemporary French and English cosmetics advertising discourse. The language of cosmetics advertising is a topical subject that has not yet merited book-length attention. It has been the sole focus of a small number of journal articles and edited book chapters (notably Coupland 2003, 2007; Lazar 2006, 2011; Harrison 2008, 2012; Ringrow 2014). Elsewhere, examples of cosmetics advertising language have been considered to some extent within broader research on female media discourse (see for example Benwell and Stokoe 2006; Jeffries 2007). This book aims to contribute to the existing literature by offering a focused analysis of cosmetics advertisements. The impetus for the cross-cultural element of this research has been driven by the small number of English/French comparative critical approaches to advertising data (one exception being Kuhn and Lick's (2009) exploration of a coffee creamer advertisement in English- versus French-speaking Canada).[9] Another motivation for this research is the hope that feminist linguistic studies may help the analyst to discover and challenge naturalised gendered assumptions in female-targeted media discourse. In doing so, the book also explores the differences and/or similarities between English and French cosmetics advertising discourse in the data analysed. It also proposes a new model of Problem-Solution patterning (Hoey 1983, 2001) for specific application to English and French cosmetics advertisements.

The data used in this book are cosmetics advertisements[10] that were collected over a period of five months from May to September 2011 (inclusive). The advertisements were sourced from glossy women's magazines, for the straightforward reason that advertisements often account for 50 % of their content (Gill 2007: 181). *Cosmopolitan* and *Elle* magazines[11] were selected because they both have British English and Metropolitan French editions. They are representative of a particular genre of women's magazines (the 'glossy') with broadly similar demographics, content, and style. There are, however, some minor differences between the two publications. *Cosmopolitan* is in many ways the prototypical women's glossy, with an almost infamous focus on sex and relationships,[12] whereas *Elle* has a greater emphasis on fashion and beauty. Both are currently owned by Hearst Magazines. The collected materials therefore provide a snapshot of contemporary Metropolitan France and British English cosmetics advertising discourse. The advertisements were stored in a corpus[13] using ATLAS.

ti software.[14] This was therefore a comparable corpus,[15] as the two datasets were collected using similar sampling techniques and are taken to be broadly representative of a particular genre, timeframe, and so on. Comparable corpora have recently been gaining popularity, especially in terms of research into femininity and sexual identity (McEnery et al. 2006: 109–111).[16]

Analytical Framework of This Study

In beauty advertising, ideological assumptions about gender are continually circulated and reinforced through discursive means as 'common sense' (Lazar 2005b: 7). This is a position that is argued throughout this book, especially in relation to how cosmetics advertising represents the 'problematic' female body and presupposes a 'need' for products to improve the female appearance. The advertisements are explored through the main analytical framework used in this study, which is that of Feminist Critical Discourse Analysis (FCDA), a term generally attributed to Lazar (2005a, 2007). FCDA critically approaches texts using linguistic methods with an overarching feminist impetus (Lazar 2005a, 2007). FCDA can perhaps most productively be viewed as a sub-discipline of Critical Discourse Analysis (CDA) as a whole, which is in very general terms an approach to language that considers its connections to power through linguistic analysis. On a macro-level, CDA (or the broader discipline sometimes known as Critical Discourse Studies) is concerned with issues of language, power, and ideology. On a micro-level, this tends to entail close linguistic analysis of texts in order to determine how certain ideologies are constructed and/ or perpetuated through chosen stretches of discourse. CDA is a wide-ranging field of research, which makes all-encompassing definitions difficult. However, a critical approach to language is a key component running though many strands of this kind of research. Lazar (2005a, 2007) argues that a more explicit feminist label can be an important step in drawing attention to gender research in CDA and may also contribute to possible collaborations between feminist linguistic scholars (Lazar 2005b: 3–4). As contemporary advertising tends to be both ever-present and highly gendered, it is well suited to FCDA research (Lazar 2007: 156, 160). CDA, and by extension FCDA, makes use of a range of tools to explore data and, as such, within each analytical chapter of the book there is a certain flexibility in the methods used. The main emphasis is on textual analysis, with some reference to the visuals in the advertisements as appropriate.[17] Statistics are used for comparative purposes to address differences and similarities in the English and French datasets.

CONTENT OF THIS BOOK

Chapter 2 outlines the research context of this study, in terms of both the existing language and gender literature and key ideas about femininity. After providing this context, Chapter 3 considers how the pursuit of Western media's youthful, perfected bodily ideal is manifested through the English and French data under analysis. This chapter adapts Hoey's (1983, 2001) model for specific application to cosmetics advertising discourse. Chapter 4 explores the media discourse of femininity as a sensual identity in beauty advertisements. The analysis in this chapter considers the various textual and visual ways in which femininity is discursively linked to a sensualised feminine identity. Chapter 5 analyses a somewhat different phenomenon: the connection of femininity with science through use of 'scientised' discourse, often in an attempt to imbue the product with a sense of authenticity. The final chapter provides a case for the use of FCDA as an analytical framework, and reflects on how it has been used in this present study.

NOTES

1. The terms 'Western' and 'Eastern' are not unproblematic, but used here as a way of signalling extremely general cultural differences.
2. I am one of them.
3. Based on data compiled from The Beauty Company, U.S. News and World Report, and L'Bel USA. It should be noted that figures do vary.
4. See for example Klein (2000); Lash and Lury (2007); Banet-Weiser (2012).
5. For more information, see https://www.asa.org.uk/ and http://www.arpp-pub.org/
6. See https://www.cap.org.uk/Advertising-Codes/Non-Broadcast/CodeItem. aspx?cscid=%7B71465b52-4ad3-4154-819f-04bb1690fad8%7D#. VvA5F-KdCUk; https://www.asa.org.uk/News-resources/Hot-Topics/ Health-and-beauty.aspx#.VvA5Z-KdCUk; and http://www.arpp-pub. org/reco_produits_cosmetiques.html
7. Detailed information available at https://www.asa.org.uk/News-resources/Hot-Topics/Health-and-beauty.aspx#.VvA5Z-KdCUk and http://www.arpp-pub.org/reco_produits_cosmetiques.html
8. See https://www.asa.org.uk/News-resources/Hot-Topics/Health-and-beauty.aspx#.VvA5Z-KdCUk
9. There is, however, some research that addresses mixing English in French advertising and French in English advertising from a sociolinguistic research perspective (see for example Martin 2002; Kelly-Holmes 2005).

10. With regard to what are classified as 'cosmetics' advertisements for the purposes of this study, definitions of cosmetics vary widely in popular usage, within the beauty industry (including the leading trade journals), and according to government legislation (Jones 2010: 1). Products excluded from my working definition of cosmetics included hygiene and/or 'quasi-medicinal' products, such as soaps, intimate washes, hand sanitisers, deodorants, sunscreens, acne creams, and anti-perspirants. 'Beauty tools' such as make-up brushes, false eyelashes, and hair straightening irons were excluded. Advertisements for fragrance (sometimes regarded as a cosmetic, sometimes as a related product) were omitted, largely because they contain very little text (generally just brand name and image).

11. *Elle* magazine is a weekly publication in France but monthly in the United Kingdom, and *Cosmopolitan* is a monthly publication in both the United Kingdom and France. Each month in the collection period, all cosmetics advertisements appearing in the four to five French *Elle* magazines, one *Elle* UK magazine, one *Cosmopolitan* France magazine, and one *Cosmopolitan* UK magazine were examined. A total of 495 advertisements, of which 249 were French and 246 were English, were therefore collected from a total of 35 magazines over the five-month period.

12. See Machin and Thornborrow (2003) for a critical linguistic analysis of the 'fun fearless female' portrayed in *Cosmopolitan* magazine worldwide. Demographic information for these two publications can also be found at www.ellemediakit.com and www.cosmomediakit.com

13. This study is broadly corpus-based (Tognini-Bonelli 2001), as the corpus is used to facilitate the research, and the analysis itself does not use traditional computational corpus linguistics tools.

14. This allowed for corpus tagging in terms of the researcher's own categories in addition to meta-information about a given advertisement. The tagging of different categories in the corpus was useful in terms of a form of 'pre-analysis' for qualitative explorations, in addition to facilitating later quantitative research. The advertisements were all sourced from hard copies of magazines, scanned as PDFs, and then input into the corpus in their original format (identical to the hard copy), which was beneficial in terms of gaining a 'holistic' view of the advertisement and opening up the possibility for both textual and visual analysis.

15. Unlike a parallel corpus, the sub-corpora in a comparable corpus are not direct translations of one another (McEnery et al. 2006: 48), although this corpus does contain a selection of parallel advertisements as, for example, the French and English magazines often ran the same advertisement in both languages during the timeframe of the data collection.

16. Baker (see for example 2006, 2014; Baker and Levon 2015) has been particularly interested in the methodological benefits of combining corpus linguistics with critical linguistic approaches to data, in terms of gaining different perspectives on the same dataset and facilitating triangulation of results.

17. Unfortunately the advertisements themselves cannot be reproduced due to copyright restrictions.

References

Althusser, L. (1969). Ideology and ideological state apparatuses (notes towards an investigation). In Althusser, L. (1977). *Lenin and philosophy and other essays* (Translated from the French by Brewster, B., 2nd ed., pp. 121–173). London: NLB.

Baker, P. (2006). *Using corpora in discourse analysis*. London: Continuum.

Baker, P. (2014). *Using corpora to analyse gender*. London: Bloomsbury.

Baker, P., & Levon, E. (2015). Picking the right cherries?: A comparison of corpus-based and qualitative analyses of news articles about masculinity. *Discourse and Communication, 9*(2), 221–336.

Banet-Weiser, S. (2012). *Authentic™: The politics of ambivalence in a brand culture*. New York: New York University Press.

Benwell, B., & Stokoe, E. (2006). *Discourse and identity*. Edinburgh: Edinburgh University Press.

Byerly, C., & Ross, K. (2006). *Women and media: A critical introduction*. Oxford: Blackwell.

Coupland, J. (2003). Ageist ideology and discourses of control in skincare product marketing. In J. Coupland & R. Gwyn (Eds.), *Discourse, the body and identity* (pp. 127–150). Basingstoke: Palgrave Macmillan.

Coupland, J. (2007). Gendered discourses on the 'problem' of ageing: Consumerised solutions. *Discourse and Communication, 1*(1), 37–61.

de Mooij, M. (2010). *Consumer behaviour and culture: Consequences for global marketing and advertising*. Thousand Oaks: SAGE.

Gauntlett, D. (2008). *Media, gender and identity: An introduction* (2nd ed.). London: Routledge.

Gill, R. (2007). *Gender and the media*. Cambridge: Cambridge University Press.

Greer, G. (2007). *The whole woman*. London: Transworld.

Harrison, C. (2008). Real men do wear mascara: Advertising discourse and masculine identity. *Critical Discourse Studies, 5*(1), 55–73.

Harrison, C. (2012). Studio5ive.com: Selling cosmetics to men and reconstructing masculine identity. In K. Ross (Ed.), *The handbook of gender, sex and media* (pp. 189–204). London: Wiley-Blackwell.

Hoey, M. (1983). *On the surface of discourse*. London: Allen and Unwin.

Hoey, M. (2001). *Textual interaction: An introduction to written discourse analysis*. London: Routledge.

Hollows, J. (2000). *Feminism, femininity and popular culture*. Manchester: Manchester University Press.

Jeffries, L. (2007). *The textual construction of the female body: A critical discourse analysis approach*. Basingstoke: Palgrave Macmillan.

Jones, G. (2010). *Beauty imagined: A history of the global beauty industry*. Oxford: Oxford University Press.

Kelly-Holmes, H. (2005). *Advertising as multilingual communication*. Basingstoke: Palgrave Macmillan.

Klein, N. (2000). *No logo*. New York: Picador.

Kuhn, J., & Lick, E. (2009). Advertising to Canada's official language groups: A comparative critical discourse analysis. *Semiotica, 176*(1), 165–176.

Lash, S., & Lury, C. (2007). *Global culture industry: The mediation of things*. Cambridge: Polity Press.

Lazar, M. (Ed.). (2005a). *Feminist critical discourse analysis: Gender, power and ideology in discourse*. Basingstoke: Palgrave Macmillan.

Lazar, M. (2005b). Politicising gender in discourse: Feminist critical discourse analysis as political perspective and praxis. In M. Lazar (Ed.), *Feminist critical discourse analysis: Gender, power and ideology in discourse* (pp. 1–30). Basingstoke: Palgrave Macmillan.

Lazar, M. (2006). "Discover the power of femininity!" Analysing global "power femininity" in local advertising. *Feminist Media Studies: New Femininities, 6*(4), 505–517.

Lazar, M. (2007). Feminist critical discourse analysis: Articulating a feminist discourse praxis. *Critical Discourse Studies, 1*(2), 141–164.

Lazar, M. (2011). The right to be beautiful: Postfeminist identity and consumer beauty advertising. In R. Gill & C. Scharff (Eds.), *New femininities: Postfeminism, neoliberalism and subjectivity* (pp. 37–51). Basingstoke: Palgrave Macmillan.

Machin, D., & Thornborrow, J. (2003). Branding and discourse: The case of Cosmopolitan. *Discourse and Society, 1*(4), 453–471.

Machin, D., & van Leeuwen, T. (2007). *Global media discourse: A critical introduction*. London: Routledge.

Martin, E. (2002). Mixing English in French advertising. *World Englishes, 21*(3), 375–401.

McEnery, A., Xiao, R., & Tono, Y. (2006). *Corpus-based language studies*. London: Routledge.

Mills, S. (2012). *Gender matters: Feminist linguistic analysis*. London: Equinox.

Munday, J. (2004). Advertising: Some challenges to translation theory. *The Translator, 10*(2), 199–219.

Murray, S. (2008). *The 'fat' female body*. Basingstoke: Palgrave Macmillan.

Rhode, D. (2010). *The beauty bias: The injustice of appearance in life and law.* New York: Oxford University Press.

Ringrow, H. (2014). Peptides, proteins and peeling active ingredients: Exploring 'scientific' language in English and French cosmetics advertising. *Études de Stylistique Anglaise, 7,* 183–210.

Sidiropoulou, M. (2008). Cultural encounters in advertisement translation. *Journal of Modern Greek Studies, 26*(2), 337–362.

Smith, D. (1988). Becoming feminine. In L. Roman & L. Christian-Smith (Eds.), *Becoming feminine: The politics of popular culture* (pp. 35–79). New York: Falmer Press.

Talbot, M. (2010). *Language and gender* (2nd ed.). Cambridge: Polity Press.

Tognini-Bonelli, B. (2001). *Corpus linguistics at work.* Amsterdam: John Benjamins.

Toolan, M. (1997). What is critical discourse analysis and why are people saying such terrible things about it? *Language and Literature, 6*(2), 83–103.

Walter, N. (1999). *The new feminism.* London: Virago.

Wolf, N. (1991). *The beauty myth: How images of beauty are used against women.* London: Vintage.

Woodward-Smith, E., & Eynullaeva, E. (2009). A cross-cultural study of the translation of advertisements for beauty products. *Perspectives: Studies in Translatology, 17*(2), 121–136.

CHAPTER 2

Language, Gender, and Advertising

Abstract The chapter begins by exploring how the language of beauty advertising is inherently linked to questions of language and power. Relevant language, gender, and advertising research in Anglophone and Francophone contexts is then outlined, with an emphasis on how contemporary feminist linguistic research tends to focus on the construction of gender in certain contexts. In cosmetics advertising in particular, femininity is equated with consumption in order to improve one's appearance, which is always seen as in need of 'fixing'. By examining the language of beauty advertisements, female media representation can be explored and challenged.

Keywords Gender and advertising • Cosmetics advertisements • Femininity • Advertising across cultures

DISCOURSE AND POWER

Exploring the language of beauty advertising is intrinsically connected to issues of language and power. In critical linguistic research, 'discourse' often denotes text and image in real-use contexts. The nature of discourse is multi-faceted: discourse itself constructs ideas and related meanings, and discourse is also the *medium* through which ideas and related meanings

© The Editor(s) (if applicable) and The Author(s) 2016   13
H. Ringrow, *The Language of Cosmetics Advertising*,
DOI 10.1057/978-1-137-55798-8_2

are realised and represented in a range of settings. In turn, this under-standing of discourse encompasses text production and text reception. The plural *discourses* is often employed in order to describe a particular ideological strand in one or a series of texts (van Leeuwen 2005: 95; see also Sunderland 2004).

'Discourse' is also a preferred term for critical discourse analysts in part because it helps to emphasise the connections between language and power. Power can be viewed conceptually on both individual and group levels, especially if we consider how much power individuals have in relation to wider societal structures. A common understand-ing of power regards it as privileged access to social resources such as education and wealth, which in turn gives status to one group over another (Machin and Mayr 2012: 24). In many contemporary Western societies, power generally refers not to totalitarian regimes, but to a much more nuanced and subtle form in which groups or individuals are often led to believe that another group's dominance is legitimate or legitimised (Simpson and Mayr 2010: 2). Gramsci's (1971) concept of hegemony is important here: dominant groups must keep hold of their status by making it seem 'natural'. This is often realised through the mainstream discourses of institutions such as the mass media, which may reinforce certain ideologies (defined here as representations of the world which help establish and support current power relations) in a particular socio-economic context (Chouliaraki and Fairclough 1999: 24; Fairclough 2003: 9). In the case of advertising discourse, ideolo-gies surrounding gender norms, the female body, and capitalism are reinforced through the language and imagery of many brands' market-ing materials. Ideology as embedded in particular texts does not exist in isolation but in relation to both daily life and to counter-ideologies and counter-discourses, which can productively be seen as all competing for various versions of 'truths' (Simpson and Mayr 2010: 4). Through ideologies, a range of assumptions, conventions, social mores, and pre-scribed behaviours can be seen as axiomatic (Fairclough 2015: 35). While arguably there exists 'life' outside of discourse, discourse itself is key in shaping realities and certain understandings. Critical linguistic analyses can help explore which ideologies are present in discourse: notably, whose beliefs and viewpoints are being promoted or taken for granted (Machin and Mayr 2012: 24). It should be emphasised that dominant ideologies are not fixed, but rather subject to societal and historical shifts (Bignell 2002: 25). Of course, people can challenge such assumptions in a range of ways, which connects broadly with a more Foucauldian (1977) view of power as a potentially productive site of negotiation.

LANGUAGE, GENDER, AND ADVERTISING RESEARCH

The three major historical approaches in the study of language and gender research are the Deficit, Dominance, and Difference approaches.[1] From Lakoff (1975), who discussed 'powerless' female speech characteristics, to Spender's (1980) contestations that men have created and controlled language, to the widely popularised myth that men and women speak totally different languages (Tannen 1991), all three frameworks are not without critique from methodological and theoretical standpoints.[2] Arguably none of them alone can fully represent the whole picture of language and gender (Cameron 1995), and more recent feminist linguistic work has tended to suggest a move beyond these frameworks (see for example Cameron 1998; Lazar 2005, 2011; Litosseliti 2006; Benwell and Stokoe 2006).

The term 'feminist linguistics' has been used to denote a broad range of theoretical and applied approaches. Generally, feminist linguistic frameworks investigate language in what are perceived to be 'gendered' domains, exploring stereotypical language behaviours and discovering how women (and men) actually use language (Mills 2012: 115). In general terms, different approaches in feminist linguistics can be historically linked to the wave of feminism that was prevalent at that time. Mills (2012: 115–118) makes a distinction between second wave feminist linguistics and third wave feminist linguistics: the former with a focus on women as an oppressed homogenous group; the latter challenging this simplified concept of power relations and focusing on studies of groups of females within a particular context. More recent feminist linguistic approaches have marked a change in the conceptualisation of gender, with many scholars now viewing gender as a process: a fluid and changing construct (see for example Baxter 2003, 2008, 2010; Litosseliti 2006; Cameron 2006; Benwell and Stokoe 2006). Coates (2004: 6) suggests that this dynamic, social constructionist approach to gender is the fourth major framework in feminist linguistics. It is heavily influenced by post-modernism and draws on Butler's (1990) conceptualisation of gender as *performance* and *performative*.[3] To use Eckert and McConnell-Ginet's phraseology, 'gender' is a 'dynamic verb' (1992: 462). In performing gender, we are '[...] materialising gender/sexual identity/desire by repeating, consciously or not, the acts that conventionally signify "femininity" or "butchness" or "flirting"' (Cameron and Kulick 2003: 150). As such, it could be argued that '[…] each individual subject must constantly negotiate the norms, behaviours, discourses that define masculinity and femininity for a particular community at a particular point in history' (Cameron 1995: 43). This conceptualisation of gender, however, does not mean that gender can necessarily be freely chosen: disregard for and transgression of social norms tends to entail negative social consequences. However, the importance of viewing gender in this way is that gender is problematised and gender constructs can be contested (Cameron 1995: 43).

Whilst the Deficit, Dominance, and Difference frameworks tended to focus on language *use* (particularly spoken language), more recent research (influenced by contemporary feminism) has considered the linguistic constructions and representations of different gender identities. This change can be seen as part of 'the shift to discourse' with research highlighting the discursive construction of gender (Litosseliti 2006: 47; see also Baker 2011). Thus, the constructions of femininities explored in this book can be seen as 'gendered identities' or 'gendered discourses' (Benwell and Stokoe 2006; Sunderland 2004). 'Sites' for the discursive construction of gender include the media (see Gill 2007a; Gauntlett 2008) and the workplace (see Thornborrow 2002). There has also been an increased focus on men's language and the discursive construction of masculinity in different contexts (see for example Coates 2003; Cameron and Kulick 2003; Baker 2008). Contemporary feminist linguistics aims '[…] to theorise gender-related linguistic phenomena and language use, and to explicitly link this to gender inequality or discrimination, on the assumption that linguistic change is an important part of overall social change' (Litosseliti 2006: 23). This therefore makes it possible to move beyond stereotypes as it does not primarily assume that men and women form homogenous groups speaking different languages, nor does it assume that all women have less power than men in every context. It also enables consideration of gender in relation to other social or contextual variables, as appropriate. Contemporary feminist linguistic research tends to draw on a range of approaches including, but not limited to, Critical Discourse Analysis (see Sunderland 2004; Lazar 2005, 2007; Coupland 2007); pragmatics (see Christie 2000); multimodal analysis (see Machin and Thornborrow 2003), post-structuralism (see Baxter 2003); and corpus linguistics (see Baker 2014). More generally across the theoretical and applied paradigms of gender and language research, notions of Deficit, Difference, and Dominance are giving way to a more post-modern outlook on gender as a social construction, and therefore a construction that can, and should, be challenged and resisted. In this context, feminist linguistics is concerned with the connections between language and society, with linguistic analysis being an important first step into providing insights into inequality (Mills 2012: 10).

In contrast to much Anglo-American gender and language research, in a French context, gender has often been considered as one of multiple factors (for example, along with social class or region) in a wide range of variationist sociolinguistic research, comparable to the English language tradition of researchers such as Labov (1972, 2006) and Trudgill (1974). French researchers sometimes prefer the term Gender and Language Studies (GLS) over the 'feminist linguistics' label. As part of her study on collective nouns, Tristram (2014) provides a useful critical overview of variationist sociolinguistics in France, suggesting that unlike some Anglo-American linguistic studies in which gender *has* been a significant factor, much French linguistic work has found gender to be less significant than other factors, or only significant in connection with specific variables such as age, profession, or region. In addition to variationist linguistic research, a supplementary area of French gender and language research has been on identifying and addressing sexism in the French language,[4] with a particular emphasis on lexis (including nouns and the process of noun creation). This issue is of special relevance to French as it has a grammatical gender system, which provides an additional dimension to the French sexism debate that is absent in English. Again, this issue of sexist language has also been prevalent in an Anglo-American tradition (see for example Mills 1995, 2008; Cameron 2006). Linguistic sexism research in French has also taken into consideration broader concerns such as the question of whether the French language is inherently sexist (Yaguello 1992: 98). In both French and English traditions, there has been much debate over the correlation between sexist language and sexist attitudes. What has been another language concern in French, particularly in the past three decades, is 'la féminisation des noms de métiers' (Houdebine 1992; Fleischman 1997; Dawes 2003; Conrick 2009)—that is, how to linguistically describe females who are in traditionally male-dominated professions. This debate should be situated within the context of guidelines on sexist language proffered by the French language advisory body L'Académie française,[5] which has often been opposed to la féminisation (although recommendations by L'Académie française may not always be indicative of actual usage, particularly in spoken discourse).[6]

Turning now specifically to advertising discourse, much of the earlier work on language and advertising adopted a broadly social semiotic approach, predominantly analysing print advertisements to explore how text and imagery encode certain ideological positions (Goffman 1979; Vestergaard and Schroder 1985; Williamson 1987; Kress and van Leeuwen 2006). Other scholars have applied stylistic tools to advertising text and imagery (Leech 1966; Toolan 1988; Myers 1994; Forceville 1996, 2013) and analysed pragmatic constructions (see for example Simpson 2001). Arguably the seminal work in language and advertising is Cook's (2001) monograph on the language of advertising, which provides an in-depth discourse analysis of a range of advertising texts.

We can perhaps best consider cosmetics advertising discourse as a sub-genre of advertising discourse. Much research on print-based cosmetics advertising discourse has addressed the topic as part of larger studies on magazines and/or the female body in media contexts (see for example Mills 1995; Benwell and Stokoe 2006; Jeffries 2007; Talbot 2010b). Notable exceptions include the work of Coupland, Lazar, and Harrison. Coupland (2003, 2007) focuses on the 'scientised', anti-ageing language of male and female cosmetics advertisements. Lazar (2006, 2007, 2011) analyses how beauty adverts use the language of an empowered, female identity in Singapore. Harrison (2008, 2012) applies a Systemic Functional Linguistics/Visual Social Semiotics approach to male cosmetics advertisements to investigate how 'masculinity' is carefully negotiated through this particular genre of advertising discourse to appeal to both a gay and straight demographic. Some common themes running through the research of these three scholars are the idea of the body as a site for improvement and the use of cosmetics being presented as a positive, empowering choice, which will be drawn on throughout the analysis in this book.

'Femininity' in Contemporary Media Discourse

Within a contemporary feminist linguistic paradigm, identities are conceptualised as constructs that vary greatly amongst groups and between individuals. The plural terms *femininities* and *masculinities* are therefore preferable to better capture these multiple possibilities. The term 'construct' is employed here to refer to 'construct(ions) of femininity' to reinforce the idea that femininities are media-made conceptualisations. Definitions of 'femininity' are multiple and often conflicting, which will be explored later in this section. As emphasised throughout this book, constructions of femininity may or may not correspond to actual women's experiences or lived embodiments of femininity, or, more generally, what it means to be a woman (Bignell 2002: 60). Individuals 'perform' gender, but this choice of performance is to a certain extent constrained by social norms surrounding gender and sexuality (Cameron 1995: 43). In turn, discursive practices can construct and index gender identities (see Sunderland 2004: 18). Gill (2007a) argues that conceptualisations of femininity have undergone social change and revision. She views advertising's representation of contemporary femininity as a 'bodily characteristic' compared to historical *behavioural* characteristics such as demureness, mothering skills, and so on, which may now seem old-fashioned and irrelevant to many young women (see also Gauntlett 2008: 11–13). Now, she argues, femininity is represented in advertising as 'the possession of a young, able-bodied, heterosexual, "sexy" body', which may be limiting and exclusive (Gill 2007a: 91). Although Gauntlett (2008: 11) suggests that femininity can perhaps best be characterised as an *optional* element of a contemporary female identity, in contrast to masculinity, which can be seen as the fluctuating 'state of being a man', in advertising discourse the type of femininity portrayed is often seen as normative and desirable. Advertising helps at least to sustain, if not create, these 'feminising' practices, which are not 'natural' in the sense that consumption of goods is required (Talbot 2010b: 8). Talbot (2010a: 40) cites the recent example of advertisements asking their addressee: 'are you doing enough for your underarms?', thus presupposing that addressees will be doing *something* for their underarms and may feel guilty that they are not doing more. In turn, this may help validate the purchase and usage of a product to 'treat' a certain body part, and looking after one's underarms may then perhaps become part of the 'shared wisdom' of female daily life. This might seem like a somewhat trite example, but is arguably not beyond the realms of possibility.

The consumption of cosmetic goods to improve one's appearance might correspond to Bourdieu's concept of 'cultural capital', in which objects and tastes are linked to a particular social identity that brings the user, wearer, or consumer a certain kind of power (Bourdieu 1986; Bignell 2002: 36; Machin and Thornborrow 2003: 468). In this context, 'lifestyle' can be viewed as an identity that comprises a 'real' or 'inner' self which relies on commodities to help create, reflect, develop, and sustain it (Benwell and Stokoe 2006: 171). Additionally, the notion of a 'group identity' may be created, for example, comprising all women who purchase a particular brand of skincare product or cosmetic, forming another kind of 'consumption community' as an alternative or supplement to a real-life community (Fairclough 2015: 203; see also Talbot 2010b: 107). To belong to such a community, one needs to meet the two key requirements within this neo-capitalist context: be female, and consume products (Talbot 2010b: 107). More specifically, cosmetics advertising discourse helps sustain a gendered market for certain consumer products, perpetuating 'a discourse of gender differences' (Sunderland 2004). 'Men' and 'women' are thus identified as homogenous groups for the purposes of advertising, with the ever-growing male-targeted cosmetics market preferring a slightly different approach (Benwell and Stokoe 2006: 171; Harrison 2008, 2012; Talbot 2010b: 107). The market segregation of men's and women's lifestyle magazines helps perpetuate and sustain a gender difference ideology, presupposing that the two sexes have such different preoccupations that separate magazines are required, fostering the creation of these consumption communities.

Femininity and consumption are generally linked in a way that masculinity and consumption are not, which reinforces this 'gender differences' discourse (Sunderland 2004), although there is of course the future potential for this to change somewhat as the male cosmetics market continues to expand. The main construct of femininity found in cosmetics advertising discourse is that of Commodified Femininity (Benwell and Stokoe 2006) or Consumer Femininity (Talbot 2010b): a femininity that presupposes and promotes individual consumption of beauty products as a worthwhile pursuit and expense. Femininity is equated with consumerism in large part because of economic necessity: magazines are dependent on advertising revenue.[7] Talbot (2010a: 140) points out that the average £3–4 price tag of the typical women's glossy in the UK does not even cover the paper it is printed on. Consumption is heavily embedded into the fabric of the contemporary women's magazine in a contemporary Western neo-capitalist context, chiefly through advertisements, which often account for 50 % of the content (Gill 2007a: 181), but also in advertorials and articles, which promote products in order to attract and retain high-profile advertisers (see also Goldman 1992: 136). The reliance of women's magazine publications on advertising revenue somewhat restricts the differing 'voices' on advertising in this medium, as critical viewpoints are to a certain extent eliminated (Talbot 2010a: 146).

In cosmetics advertisements, femininity tends to be idealised in that the advertisements display '[…] the juxtaposition of an impossibly flawless complexion (unattainable) and a lipstick product (attainable)' (Benwell and Stokoe 2006: 172). The body is also fragmented or itemised into parts, which, following the Problem-Solution format of advertisements, require 'fixing' or 'beauty work' (Smith 1988; Benwell and Stokoe 2006: 172; Jeffries 2007; Talbot 2010b: 136–140). These 'solutions' are not permanent: repeat purchases are required (Benwell and Stokoe 2006: 176; this is discussed further in Chapter 3). Consumer/Commodified Femininity is 'characterised by self-indulgence and narcissism' and this is reflected by the use of affective language that connects beauty products to sensuality (Benwell and Stokoe 2006: 173). Benwell and Stokoe identify nine 'rules' of this Consumer/Commodified Femininity ideology:

> 1. Ageing is bad and must be striven against or disguised; 2. Fat is bad; 3. Activity/Fitness is good, and we are always busy; 4. But inactivity in the form of relaxation or 'indulgence' is equally encouraged; 5. Body hair (except on head) is bad; 6. Natural body odour is bad, synthetic fragrance is preferable; 7. Bare face (that is, no make-up) is bad, but simultaneously a 'natural' look is prized in all arenas; 8. Transformation, newness and change are good; and 9. Consistency of appearance is good: deodorant must last, lipstick must not smudge or fade, mascara must not run, hair colour must not fade and skin must look 'even' (2006: 174–175).

These 'rules' can be linked to the overarching ideology of Consumer/ Commodified Femininity, in which appearance is prioritised and a certain look can be achieved through consumption, which will be discussed at various points in Chapters 3, 4, and 5.

The connections between this construct of Consumer/Commodified Femininity and feminism[8] are rather complex. In Consumer/Commodified Femininity, feminist values such as independence, choice, self-worth, and liberation are used often as 'commodity signs' to promote individual consumption, a process Goldman (1992) terms Commodity Feminism. Depoliticised and stripped of its overall social and emancipatory goals, feminism becomes '[…] just another style decision' (Gill 2007a: 95). Another way in which advertisers directly draw on feminist ideas is through the use of feminist (or feminist-sounding) discourse in their adverts (Gill 2007a: 94). Goldman (1992: 131) argues that '[…] sign equivalents are thus made to stand for, and made equivalent to, feminist goals of independence and professional success', with Commodity Feminism suggesting that control over one's appearance may produce positive reactions at home and at work (Goldman 1992: 153). In addition, feminism is equated to a certain extent with narcissistic tendencies when it is used in advertising discourse (Douglas 1995: 249–268; Douglas cites *L'Oréal*'s 'Because you're worth it' tagline). Mills and Mullany equate the importance of individual consumption with a 'post-feminist'[9] culture, arguing that this focus on the individual in consumerist culture obscures issues of wider social inequalities (2011: 12). Advertising agencies and brands themselves have been accused of 'co-opting' feminist standpoints into their advertising discourse for commercial gain in order to help make Consumer/Commodified Femininity more palatable to the female consumer. Whether the magazines or advertisements themselves may actually be supporting feminist values or whether they are simply using them for commercial gain in a changing cultural landscape is an area that has attracted some debate (Gill 2007a: 94–95, 202). If feminism has been used to achieve consumerist goals, this does not automatically render all progressive representations of women in advertising worthless, but such representations must be considered extremely carefully within their appropriate socio-economic context (Gill 2007a: 202; Lazar 2006: 506).

Similar to Consumer/Commodified Femininity, Lazar (2006) uses the term Power Femininity to denote 'an empowered and/or powerful feminine identity' in her study of cosmetics advertising in Singapore. This type of identity promotes a certain post-feminist interpretation of the world: feminism has achieved everything it set out to and in this new context of equality women can do whatever they desire. In particular, they can focus their energies on beautification (Lazar 2006: 505–506). In this discourse of beauty empowerment, women are granted agency to change their physical appearance through transformative action (such as in advertisements that urge them to reveal their true beauty through use of a foundation) or by resistive action, which often draws upon a metaphorical discourse of warfare such as 'fight the five major signs of ageing!' (Lazar 2006). Power Femininity, then, could perhaps be viewed as a combination of Consumer/Commodified Femininity and Commodity Feminism. Lazar also uses the term Choice Feminism (generally attributed to Hirshman 2006[10] to discuss issues surrounding stay-at-home mothers) to emphasise the connections made by advertisers not only between self-aestheticisation and femininity, but self-aestheticisation and *feminism* (Lazar 2011: 37). Thus, an emancipated feminine identity incorporates the freedom to be beautiful with the freedom to choose particular processes of beautification (Lazar 2011: 37–39). The crux of Choice Feminism is that 'choice' is inherently positive and inherently feminist (Hirshman 2006; Zeisler 2008). Many feminist scholars suggest that 'choice' has now become a synonym for 'feminism', criticising this line of reasoning and arguing that these kinds of choices are often not remotely feminist. In fact, some of these choices restrict women within a patriarchal society and further subject them to sexist societal norms (see related discussions in Hirshman 2006; Zeisler 2008; McRobbie 2009; Mendes 2012). Some scholars argue that the concept of choice has been completely depoliticised, originating from debates surrounding a woman's right to have an abortion but now being applied to the choice to consume (Zeisler 2008: 131–132; Lazar 2011: 40–44). In the rhetoric of cosmetics marketing, an example of a salient choice women may be making is which skin-flattering shade of bronzer to purchase (see Lazar 2011: 43–44). The only choice not offered to women in this discourse is the one *not* to consume: to opt out of compliance with the commercialised beauty rituals and ideals (Lazar 2011: 45).[11]

Exploring Gendered Language

Language and gender research has therefore seen a move away from potentially essentialist research on female-male differences to new kinds of approaches that focus on gendered language in different contexts, such as the discourse of female-targeted cosmetics advertising explored in this book. By examining these kinds of 'gendered discourses' (Sunderland 2004), we can address questions of representations of the female body and femininity in different cultural and linguistic contexts. The concept of Consumer/Commodified Femininity provides a useful backdrop in this context of analysing language to 'unmask the politics of everyday life' (Crawford 1995: 180). The following chapters will focus on how linguistic strategies used in French and English cosmetics advertising contribute to this kind of femininity construction.

Notes

1. In 1922 Danish linguist Jespersen presented an outline of women's 'deficient' language in his book *Language: Its Nature and Development*. However, since his work did not have a critical impetus and was very much a product of its time with regard to its explicit sexism, it cannot be easily classified under the umbrella of 'feminist linguistics'. Lakoff's work is therefore generally viewed as marking the beginning of language and gender studies proper. Nonetheless, the fact that 'women's language' warranted a chapter in Jespersen's book at all was rather radical within its historical and social context.
2. See Talbot (2010a) and Baker (2011) for comprehensive critical overviews of these frameworks; see Cameron (2008) for discussion of popular language and gender myths.

3. This notion of gender as performance has been influenced by Queer Theory, which posits that identities are not fixed. For more on the connections between Queer Theory and gender identity, see Schor and Weed (1997).

4. In addition to the two strands of gender and language research mentioned here, Marnette (2005) considers the language used in contemporary women's press as part of her stylistics research on Speech and Thought Presentation (S&TP) in French. She explores the connections between the 'théorie de l'énonciation' and S&TP in French, applying these frameworks to French women's magazine discourse, investigating how the publications attempt to identify with the reader through S&TP strategies, notably through first-person narrative accounts of anonymous readers.

5. See http://www.academie-francaise.fr

6. The examples mentioned here are from Metropolitan French and are not necessarily indicative of all French- speaking countries or regions. Québec, for example, has taken a more proactive approach in feminising job titles by creating new female forms for many professions. For example, 'une professeure' (a female teacher) is currently widespread in Québec but is not the norm for usage in mainland France (see Conrick 2009). As a counter-example, the French term for university lecturer, 'le maître/la maîtresse', appears to resist la féminisation, both inside and outside of la Métropole.

7. Similarly, Glapka (2014) identifies a type of 'bridal femininity' found in UK wedding magazines, in which gym memberships, skincare, make-up, and a range of other modes of consumption help to ensure a 'perfect day', with clear connections between the advertising and magazine articles.

8. The plural *feminisms* is perhaps more reflective of the current range of theories and practices. For the purposes of this book, I prefer the broad definition of feminism given by Cameron and Kulick (2003: 52): 'Feminism is a political movement concerned with advancing the interests of women, and the key social relation it theorises is gender'.

9. Post-feminism can be understood in a range of ways, often as a new stage of society in which feminism is viewed as irrelevant and/or as a backlash against previous waves of feminism (see for example McRobbie 2009; Mendes 2012; for media representations of post-feminism see Gill 2007b).

10. See also http://prospect.org/article/homeward-bound-0

11. Of relevance here is the additional concept of Hegemonic Femininity (Schippers 2007). Schippers builds on Connell's (1987, 2005) concept of Hegemonic Masculinity, characterised as the gender practice '[…] which combines the culturally accepted answer to the problem of the legitimacy of the patriarchy which guarantees (or is taken to guarantee) the dominant position of men and the subordination of women' (Connell 2005: 77).

This form of masculinity is reinforced through societal structures such as the mass media. Connell (1987: 183) argues that whilst many femininities exist, there is no Hegemonic Femininity to rival that of Hegemonic Masculinity. Schippers (2007) takes issue with this line of thought and argues *for* the existence of Hegemonic Femininity, which fits into the existing paradigm and from which we can then identify deviant 'pariah' femininities: lesbians, 'promiscuous' women, aggressive females, and so on.

REFERENCES

Baker, P. (2008). *Sexed texts: Language, gender and sexuality.* London: Equinox.

Baker, P. (2011). Discourse and gender. In K. Hyland & B. Paltridge (Eds.), *The continuum companion to discourse analysis* (pp. 199–212). London: Continuum.

Baker, P. (2014). *Using corpora to analyse gender.* London: Bloomsbury.

Baxter, J. (2003). *Positioning gender in discourse: A feminist methodology.* Basingstoke: Palgrave Macmillan.

Baxter, J. (2008). Feminist post-structuralist discourse analysis: A new theoretical and methodological approach. In K. Harrington, L. Litosseliti, H. Sauntson, & J. Sunderland (Eds.), *Gender and language research methodologies* (pp. 243–255). Basingstoke: Palgrave Macmillan.

Baxter, J. (2010). Discourse-analytical approaches to text and talk. In L. Litosseliti (Ed.), *Research methods in linguistics* (pp. 117–137). London: Continuum.

Benwell, B., & Stokoe, E. (2006). *Discourse and identity.* Edinburgh: Edinburgh University Press.

Bignell, J. (2002). *Media semiotics: An introduction* (2nd ed.). Manchester: Manchester University Press.

Bourdieu, P. (1986). The forms of capital. In J. Richardson (Ed.), *The handbook of theory and research for the sociology of education* (pp. 241–258). New York: Greenwood.

Butler, J. (1990). *Gender trouble: Feminism and the subversion of identity.* New York: Routledge.

Cameron, D. (1995). Rethinking language and gender studies: Some issues for the 1990s. In S. Mills (Ed.), *Language and gender: Interdisciplinary perspectives* (pp. 31–44). London: Longman.

Cameron, D. (Ed.). (1998). *The feminist critique of language: A reader* (2nd ed.). London: Routledge.

Cameron, D. (2006). *On language and sexual politics.* London: Routledge.

Cameron, D. (2008). *The myth of Mars and Venus.* Oxford: Oxford University Press.

Cameron, D., & Kulick, D. (2003). *Language and sexuality.* Cambridge: Cambridge University Press.

Chouliaraki, L., & Fairclough, N. (1999). *Discourse in late modernity: Rethinking critical discourse analysis.* Edinburgh: Edinburgh University Press.

Christie, C. (2000). *Gender and language: Towards a feminist pragmatics.* Edinburgh: Edinburgh University Press.

Coates, J. (2003). *Men talk: Stories in the making of masculinities.* Oxford: Blackwell.

Coates, J. (2004). *Women, men and language: A sociolinguistic account of gender differences in language* (3rd ed.). Harlow: Pearson Education.

Connell, R. (1987). *Gender and power: Society, the person and sexual politics.* Cambridge: Polity Press.

Connell, R. (2005). *Masculinities.* Berkeley: University of California Press.

Conrick, M. (2009). Representations of gender in the francophone context of Québec and Canada: *la féminisation linguistique* in principle and practice. *International Journal of Canadian Studies/Revue Internationale d'Études Canadiennes, 48,* 121–133.

Cook, G. (2001). *The discourse of advertising* (2nd ed.). London: Routledge.

Coupland, J. (2003). Ageist ideology and discourses of control in skincare product marketing. In J. Coupland & R. Gwyn (Eds.), *Discourse, the body and identity* (pp. 127–150). Basingstoke: Palgrave Macmillan.

Coupland, J. (2007). Gendered discourses on the 'problem' of ageing: Consumerised solutions. *Discourse and Communication, 1*(1), 37–61.

Crawford, M. (1995). *Talking difference: On gender and language.* London: SAGE.

Dawes, E. (2003). La féminisation des titres et fonctions dans la Francophonie: de la morphologie à l'idéologie. *Ethnologies, 25*(2), 195–217.

Douglas, S. (1995). *Where the girls are: Growing up female with the mass media.* New York: Penguin Books USA.

Eckert, P., & McConnell-Ginet, S. (1992). Think practically and look locally: Language and gender as community-based practice. *Annual Review of Anthropology, 21,* 461–490.

Fairclough, N. (2003). *Analysing discourse: Textual analysis for social research.* London: Routledge.

Fairclough, N. (2015). *Language and power* (3rd ed.). Harlow: Longman.

Fleischman, S. (1997). The battle of feminism and *bon usage:* Instituting nonsexist usage in French. *The French Review, 70*(6), 834–844.

Forceville, C. (1996). *Pictorial metaphor in advertising.* London: Routledge.

Forceville, C. (2013). The strategic use of the visual mode in advertising metaphors. In E. Djonov & S. Zhao (Eds.), *Critical multimodal studies of popular culture* (pp. 55–70). New York: Routledge.

Foucault, M. (1977). *Discipline and punish: The Birth of the prison* (Translated from the French by Sheridan, A.). London: Allen Lane.

Gauntlett, D. (2008). *Media, gender and identity: An introduction* (2nd ed.). London: Routledge.

Gill, R. (2007a). *Gender and the media.* Cambridge: Cambridge University Press.

Gill, R. (2007b). Postfeminist media culture: Elements of a sensibility. *European Journal of Cultural Studies, 10*(2), 147–166.

Glapka, E. (2014). *Reading bridal magazines from a critical discursive perspective.* Basingstoke: Palgrave Macmillan.

Goffman, E. (1979). *Gender advertisements.* London: Macmillan.

Goldman, R. (1992). *Reading ads socially.* London/New York: Routledge.

Gramsci, A. (1971). *Selections from the prison notebooks.* London: Lawrence and Wishart.

Harrison, C. (2008). Real men do wear mascara: Advertising discourse and masculine identity. *Critical Discourse Studies, 5*(1), 55–73.

Harrison, C. (2012). Studio5ive.com: Selling cosmetics to men and reconstructing masculine identity. In K. Ross (Ed.), *The handbook of gender, sex and media* (pp. 189–204). London: Wiley-Blackwell.

Hirshman, L. (2006). *Get to work: A manifesto for women of the world.* New York: Viking.

Houdebine, A. M. (1992). Sur la féminisation des noms de métiers en France. *Recherches féministes, 5*(1), 153–159.

Jeffries, L. (2007). *The textual construction of the female body: A critical discourse analysis approach.* Basingstoke: Palgrave Macmillan.

Jespersen, O. (1922). *Language: Its nature, development and origin.* London: George Allen and Unwin Ltd.

Kress, G., & van Leeuwen, T. (2006). *Reading images: The grammar of visual design* (2nd ed.). London: Routledge.

Labov, W. (1972). *Sociolinguistic patterns.* Philadelphia: Pennsylvania Press, Inc.

Labov, W. (2006). *The social stratification of English in New York city* (2nd ed.). New York: Cambridge University Press.

Lakoff, R. (1975). *Language and woman's place.* New York: Harper and Row.

Lazar, M. (Ed.). (2005). *Feminist critical discourse analysis: Gender, power and ideology in discourse.* Basingstoke: Palgrave Macmillan.

Lazar, M. (2006). "Discover the power of femininity!" Analysing global "power femininity" in local advertising. *Feminist Media Studies: New Femininities, 6*(4), 505–517.

Lazar, M. (2007). Feminist critical discourse analysis: Articulating a feminist discourse praxis. *Critical Discourse Studies, 1*(2), 141–164.

Lazar, M. (2011). The right to be beautiful: Postfeminist identity and consumer beauty advertising. In R. Gill & C. Scharff (Eds.), *New femininities: Postfeminism, neoliberalism and subjectivity* (pp. 37–51). Basingstoke: Palgrave Macmillan.

Leech, G. (1966). *English in advertising: A linguistic study of advertising in Great Britain.* London: Longman.

Litosseliti, L. (2006). *Gender and language: Theory and practice.* London: Hodder Arnold.

Machin, D., & Mayr, A. (2012). *How to do critical discourse analysis: A multi-modal introduction*. London: SAGE.

Machin, D., & Thornborrow, J. (2003). Branding and discourse: The case of Cosmopolitan. *Discourse and Society, 1*(4), 453–471.

Marnette, S. (2005). *Speech and thought presentation in French: Concepts and strategies*. Amsterdam: John Benjamins.

McRobbie, A. (2009). *The aftermath of feminism: Gender, culture and social change*. London: SAGE.

Mendes, K. (2012). "Feminism rules! Now, where's my swimsuit?" Re-evaluating feminist discourse in print media 1968–2008. *Media, Culture & Society, 34*(5), 554–570.

Mills, S. (1995). *Feminist stylistics*. London: Routledge.

Mills, S. (2008). *Language and sexism*. Cambridge: Cambridge University Press.

Mills, S. (2012). *Gender matters: Feminist linguistic analysis*. London: Equinox.

Mills, S., & Mullany, L. (2011). *Language, gender and feminism: Theory, methodology and practice*. London: Routledge.

Myers, G. (1994). *Words in ads*. London: Edward Arnold.

Schippers, M. (2007). Recovering the feminine other: Masculinity, femininity, and gender hegemony. *Theory and Society, 36*, 85–102.

Schor, N., & Weed, E. (Eds.). (1997). *Feminism meets queer theory*. Bloomington/Indianapolis: Indiana University Press.

Simpson, P. (2001). 'Reason' and 'Tickle' as pragmatic constructs in the discourse of advertising. *Journal of Pragmatics, 33*(4), 589–607.

Simpson, P., & Mayr, A. (2010). *Language and power*. London: Routledge.

Smith, D. (1988). Becoming feminine. In L. Roman & L. Christian-Smith (Eds.), *Becoming feminine: The politics of popular culture* (pp. 35–79). New York: Falmer Press.

Spender, D. (1980). *Man made language* (1st ed.). London: Routledge and Kegan Paul.

Sunderland, J. (2004). *Gendered discourses*. Basingstoke: Palgrave Macmillan.

Talbot, M. (2010a). *Language and gender* (2nd ed.). Cambridge: Polity Press.

Talbot, M. (2010b). *Language, intertextuality and subjectivity: Voices in the construction of consumer femininity*. Saarbrücken: Lambert Academic Publishing.

Tannen, D. (1991). *You just don't understand: Men and women in conversation*. London: Viagro.

Thornborrow, J. (2002). *Power talk: Language and interaction in institutional discourse*. Essex: Pearson Education.

Toolan, M. (1988). The language of press advertising. In M. Ghadessy (Ed.), *Registers of written English* (pp. 52–64). London: Pinter.

Tristram, A. (2014). *Variation and change in French morphosyntax: The case of collective nouns*. Oxford: Legenda.

Trudgill, P. (1974). *The social differentiation of English in Norwich.* Cambridge: Cambridge University Press.

van Leeuwen, T. (2005). *Introducing social semiotics.* London: Routledge.

Vestergaard, T., & Schroder, K. (1985). *The language of advertising.* London: Blackwell.

Williamson, J. (1987). *Decoding advertisements.* London: Marion Boyars.

Yaguello, M. (1992). *Les mots et les femmes: essai d'approche socio-linguistique de la condition féminine.* Paris: Editions Payot.

Zeisler, A. (2008). *Feminism and pop culture.* Berkley: Seal Press.

CHAPTER 3

Problems and Solutions: Pursuing the Youthful, Ideal Body

Abstract Many contemporary cosmetics advertisements display a pattern commonly known as the Problem-Solution pattern (Hoey, On the surface of discourse. Allen and Unwin, London, 1983; Textual interaction: an introduction to written discourse analysis. Routledge, London, 2001) in which the beauty product is presented as a 'solution' to a 'problem' apparently faced by the target consumer. Within the context of the media pressure on females to fit into strict beauty ideals, this chapter explores how cosmetics are discursively constructed as 'tools' to help achieve an improved appearance. Hoey's Problem-Solution model is adapted for specific application to cosmetics advertising discourse, comparing how this pattern manifests itself in UK versus French advertisements.

Keywords Problem-Solution pattern • Cosmetics advertisements • Advertising across cultures

'Solutions' for the Ageing Female Body

Many advertisements display a discursive pattern commonly known as the Problem-Solution pattern (Hoey 1983, 2001) in which the product is presented as a 'solution' to a 'problem' apparently faced by the consumer. In the domain of beauty advertising, this problem tends to be an element of the female appearance: flat hair, wrinkled eyes, blemished cheeks, and so on. In a mediascape in which women are bombarded with a range of sometimes conflicting messages about their appearance and body image,[1] the Problem-Solution pattern takes as its starting point that the female body is in some way inadequate and a solution can be found for that particular inadequacy through an appropriate cosmetic product. The female consumer may not necessarily always recognise the criticism of one's body inherent in the adverts but instead participate in purchasing the solutions offered, thus '[…] becoming the moving and enthusiastic actor in [her] own self-improvement programme' (Orbach 2010: 92). As more and more problems are identified and purchasable solutions provided, what constitutes 'acceptable' female appearance may become even narrower, but this tends to be positively framed as an opportunity for continual improvement of one's appearance (Orbach 2010: 90). This self-improvement often involves an attempt to delay or disguise visual signifiers of ageing, which are constructed as inherently negative and in need of 'youthinising' (Nelson 2012: 143). In many media contexts, older women are somewhat invisible or stereotyped, and, with some exceptions,[2] are not portrayed as sexually attractive (Woodward 1991; Chivers 2003; Gill 2007a: 84–91; Hurd Clarke 2011; Nelson 2012). Beauty advertising discourse tends to presume that women should be proactive in seeking solutions for the physical effects of ageing on their faces and bodies, in addition to any other aesthetic concerns (Coupland 2003, 2007; Wykes and Gunter 2005). This ties in with the broader concept of femininity discussed earlier in the book: Consumer/Commodified Femininity (Talbot 2010b; Benwell and Stokoe 2006), which is the connection made between a certain kind of feminine identity and consumerism. In this particular context, looking younger is apparently attained through purchase and usage of various anti-ageing cosmetics. The solutions presented frequently emphasise connections to science (discussed further in Chapter 5; see also Coupland 2003). The problems are defined as such within the current social context: as youth continues to be privileged in many respects, the physical manifestations of getting older are undesirable (Sontag 1972). In beauty advertising in particular, the physical manifestations of ageing on the female face and body are generally presented as negative and in need of remedy, reinforcing 'the unwatchability of old age' (Woodward 1991; Wolf 1991: 106; Coupland 2003: 147, 2007: 43). Benwell and Stokoe (2006: 174) describe one of the 'rules' of Consumer/Commodified Femininity as 'ageing is bad and must be striven against or disguised: skin must be smooth, hair must be non-grey and bodies must be slim, supple, toned and erect'. Therefore, the solutions presented in advertising discourse provide antidotes to the varied and extensive problems of ageing.

These antidotes have so far been located mainly within the female domain. The male cosmetics market is expanding as men grow increasingly interested in cosmetics (and/or as brands provide and market more products for the male consumer), but female-targeted beauty products still dominate (Rhode 2010: 32). Typically, male-targeted advertisements have traditionally focused less on anti-ageing and more on aspects such as 'refreshing skin' and 'avoiding shine', preferring different colour schemes than those typical of female cosmetics advertisements (Benwell and Stokoe 2006: 190–193; Simpson and Mayr 2010: 89–93). Where ageing *is* mentioned in male cosmetics advertisements, it is not necessarily constructed in the same manner as in female advertisements; for example, 'expression lines' are sometimes used in place of 'wrinkles' (Coupland 2007: 48). Male beauty companies tread a fine line between differentiating their products from the women's market and focusing on how they contribute to men's overall appearance and health (Harrison 2008, 2012). Overall, men are not under the same kind of pressures as women to halt and disguise the physical signs of ageing (Sontag 1972: 32–36; Coupland 2003: 129).[3] There is a wider range of physical appearances deemed acceptable[4] for older men than for older women, and women's ageing appearance is arguably more problematised. For example, men with grey hair are frequently regarded as more attractive[5] than their female counterparts: for women, grey hair is presented as something to be disguised and there is rarely a celebration of the physical effects of ageing presented in different contexts (Woodward 1991: 32). Sontag (1972: 33) links this 'double standard' to females becoming 'less sexually desirable earlier than their male counterparts', which is arguably still true today, although of course sexual desirability is often to do with more than appearance.

Within the context of the media pressure on females to fit into strict beauty ideals, this chapter will consider how cosmetics are discursively constructed as helpful tools to achieve the youthful, perfected bodily ideal in French and English cosmetics advertisements. Hoey's (1983, 2001) Problem-Solution model will be adapted for specific application to cosmetics advertising discourse. The Problem-Solution pattern in cosmetics advertising both creates and affirms a notion of femininity that can be continually improved by use and purchase of beauty products.

THE PROBLEM-SOLUTION PATTERN (HOEY 1983, 2001)

The Problem-Solution pattern has been identified and explored most extensively in a linguistic framework by Michael Hoey (1983, 2001). By 'pattern', Hoey (1983: 31) clarifies that this noun is used to denote 'a combination of relations organising (part of) a discourse'. The basic structure of a Problem-Solution pattern is outlined below (Fig. 3.1).

The Problem-Solution pattern does not always follow the model in a linear fashion. The pattern can be multi-layered and/or may begin with the Response (Solution) instead of the Problem. The optional Situation is the element that precedes the Problem. In the following example: 'We were all out at sea. The boat sank', the first sentence here fulfils the element of Situation. However, this Situation is optional and may often be absent (Hoey 2001: 140). For example, if the text began with 'The boat sank', it would therefore commence at the Problem stage. In the Problem-Solution pattern, evaluative lexis with particular connotations is used to signal the Problem and Solution aspects. In the Problem stage, this signalling could involve the noun 'problem' itself. It could also include something encoded as such or implied to be problematic, such as 'no money', 'mess', 'difficulty', or in the above example, 'the boat sank' (Hoey 2001: 140–141). We can draw a distinction here between a Problem that is constructed using inscribed appraisal (explicitly encoded evaluation), such as 'horrible news' or 'dangerous places', and evoked appraisal (implicitly

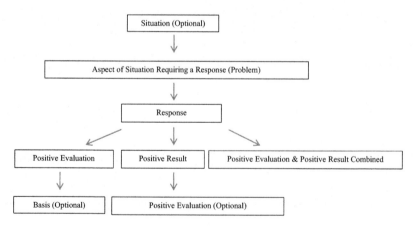

Fig. 3.1   The Problem-Solution pattern (Hoey 1983: 31, 2001: 127)

encoded evaluation) that could evoke a negative evaluation with reference to convention, such as 'a seminar that lasts longer than the allocated time' (Martin and White 2005).[6] Hoey cautions that the Problem is one which is identified as such in the text. This may overlap with or correspond to a problem in the 'real world', that is, outside of the discursive event, but it should be emphasised that this does not have to be the case (Hoey 1983: 52). In terms of beauty advertising, this is important to emphasise: is 'flat hair', for example, always a problem outside of the discourse itself? These kinds of problems identified in beauty advertising discourse may or may not be already regarded as a problem by the target consumer.

After the Problem is discursively identified, we move to the Response (Solution) stage, which can take the form of a Positive Evaluation, Positive Result or, as is often the case, the two combined, for example: 'Luckily, Bill was able to repair the boat and so we had a smooth sailing back to the shore in time for dinner'. The optional Basis for Evaluation can be used to provide some kind of evidence for the Evaluation. To use Hoey's (1983: 79) example, if the Positive Evaluation is 'The air-cushion system assures a safe and soft landing', the Basis could be 'Trials have been carried out with freight-dropping at rates of from 19 feet to 42 feet per second in winds of 49 feet per second. The charge weighed about one and a half tons'. In this example, 'been carried out' and 'weighed' indicate a past tense but the information may also prove useful for the present, while 'trials' denotes an attempt at providing evidence (Hoey 1983: 79). If a pattern includes a Negative Result or Evaluation, this may lead to the pattern recycling until a Positive Result is achieved. In the boat example, the possible Positive Result 'a man came to repair the boat' may then be overridden by a Negative Evaluation such as 'However, the patch on the boat was leaky', and so the cycle could begin again (Hoey 2001: 141).

Hoey (2001: 127) identifies additional, optional intermediate stages between Problem and Response that are not part of the model. One of these is a 'Plan', such as 'She needs to be taught a lesson' or 'I have a plan', which in a sense introduces the Response. Additionally, there can be a 'Recommended Response', such as 'I know what to do—we should phone someone for help!' The actual Response in these examples is likely to come later, when the proposed action takes place. Hoey argues that in practice many Responses in advertising discourse are actually true Recommended Responses, but '[...] in these contexts they are not felt to be interim and the actual Responses are likewise not felt to be missing' (2001: 128). It is understood that the advertiser is suggesting their particular shampoo, face cream, and so on as the *preferred* Response over others on the market.

Hoey (1983: 81–82) emphasises that the Solution and its evaluation are not inherently positive, although the term 'solution' itself in other contexts often has positive connotations and this is generally the case when Problem-Solution patterns occur in advertising discourse. Overall, Problems and Solutions are identified here through use of lexis with particular connotations: negative for the Problem and positive for the Solution (Benwell and Stokoe 2006: 177–178).

A range of research on female-targeted media discourse makes reference to Hoey's (1983, 2001) Problem-Solution pattern; however, many scholars do so in a more general sense and do not tend to analyse advertisements according to each stage of Hoey's pattern. Benwell and Stokoe (2006) explore the phenomenon of the Problem-Solution pattern with particular reference to beauty advertising in the context of commodified feminine identities. They focus on the lexical signals in the pattern to connote problems and solutions, providing examples of these in contemporary cosmetics advertising discourse, and arguing that implicature is often key in considering what is being constructed as a problem and what is being constructed as a solution (Benwell and Stokoe 2006: 177–178). Femininity tends to be idealised in the Problem-Solution pattern in advertising, which may feature an attainable product with an often unattainable image (Benwell and Stokoe 2006: 172). In a similar vein, Talbot (2010b) refers to Problem-Solution discourses in a more general sense in her analysis of female magazine discourse. She explores the 'classificatory areas' of female appearance: areas that are seen to require 'appropriate' products and solutions (Talbot 2010b: 133). These 'areas' are often constructed as various 'problems', which can include hair-growing stages and skin tone (perhaps not previously seem as problematic). Additionally, Jeffries' (2007) research addresses the Problem-Solution pattern in magazine discourse, with magazines often containing similar ideological viewpoints to the advertisements themselves. Jeffries suggests that the female body, in many of her examples, was presented as problematic and negative, whilst the solutions provided by the magazine (in the form of advice given) were lexically signalled as having positive connotations. She argues that the basic pattern of Problem paired with Solution is so prevalent in contemporary female-targeted media discourse that the creation and representation of alternative structures can be difficult (Jeffries 2007: 85). Similarly, Mills (1995) analyses the pragmatics of hair-removal products, discussing how advertisers offer a specific Solution for an identified Problem. Of course, in many kinds of media discourses the female body is seen as problematic and consumerised solutions are promoted as the appropriate answers (Wolf 1991; Rhode 2010; Orbach 2010).

A Proposed Model of Problem-Solution Patterning in Advertising Discourse

This chapter offers an adaptation of Hoey's Problem-Solution pattern for specific application to cosmetics advertising discourse. Elements of Benwell and Stokoe's (2006) Commodified Femininity discourse have been incorporated as appropriate, as will be explained shortly. A schema for the new model is produced below (Fig. 3.2).

The adapted model begins with the optional Situation. The next stage is the Situation Requiring a Response, that is, the Problem. As stated in the introduction to this chapter, if we consider how problems are defined in cosmetics advertising discourse, the more prevalent and perhaps more immediately obvious type of 'Problem(s)' are aspects of the female appearance that the target consumer is presumed to be unhappy about or

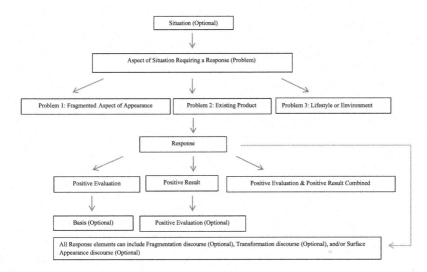

Fig. 3.2 A proposed Problem-Solution pattern for cosmetics advertising discourse

wishes to 'solve', improve, or change (Problem 1: Fragmented Aspect of Appearance). Examples could include flat hair, greasy hair, fine hair, oily skin, dry skin, crow's feet, frown lines, fine lines and wrinkles, dehydrated skin, and many, many more. These problems can be associated with ageing (**frown lines**) or with a particular skin type with various needs (**sensitive skin**) (Coupland 2007: 45). The product offers an antidote to these concerns. This category is linked to Benwell and Stokoe's (2006) concept of Fragmentation as each body part or aspect of ageing appearance is considered as a separate problem for treatment in this context. The face is a common example in this category: the face has 'heavy semiotic significance' in a Western context as it tends to always be on display (Coupland 2003: 127).

A second Problem common in cosmetics advertisements is that of issues with existing similar products on the market, or previous formulations of the same product (Problem 2: Existing Product). For example, facial creams designed to 'treat' the problem of oily skin might dry out the skin too much, which is undesirable. A new product may therefore be marketed as **controls shine without overdrying**. Often the problems with existing products can be linked to product qualities such as issues of longevity or texture (unpleasant texture, not long-lasting enough), or the product packaging (difficult to operate, not easily portable). These 'problems' may not necessarily be apparent to the consumer before they are presented in the context of solutions in advertising material, such as in the following examples: hydration **with no greasy after-feel**; pump applicator **dispenses the exact amount with no wastage**; built-in brush so **no foundation fingers**; and powder that **lasts all day with no drying effect**. The notion of a new and improved concept or product can be linked to the idea of 'newness' in consumerism in general. Consumerism itself is of course dependent upon '[…] an in-built obsolescence for products, a market requirement that newly-created 'needs' will necessitate a new product, or, for the more cynically-inclined, a newly-packaged one' (Benwell and Stokoe 2006: 176).

The third main Problem identified in the Problem-Solution pattern in cosmetics advertising discourse is what we could summarise as 'modern life', which involves lifestyle, work, stress, and the environment (Problem 3: Lifestyle or Environment). All of these factors can be represented as potentially adversely affecting the consumer's body, hair, skin, and other features. Thus, this category often draws on a discourse of *protection* against a negative entity. Benwell and Stokoe address this 'modern life' issue in their consideration of how problems are constructed:

> The consumer imperative necessitates the continual construction of problems (physical, cosmetic, emotional, lifestyle, practical) to which objects are offered as (temporary) solutions. (2006: 177)

This category often construes the target addressee as a young female in an urban, working environment. Some assumptions of this constructed Problem are:

1. Life/work/city environment/juggling job and motherhood are stressful and have negative aspects;
2. These factors can be detrimental to skin, hair, and so on;
3. Skin needs to be protected against them and/or their negative effects minimised;
4. Various cosmetics/skincare products can serve this function.

More specific examples of this problem include sleepless nights, poor diet, pollution, a busy schedule, and sun exposure, all of which are explicitly linked to undesirable effects on female appearance.

Some advertisements may use a combination of the three Problems: for example, **protect your sensitive skin** (1) **from the wind** (3) **without leaving it greasy** (2). In all three of the main problems identified, it is important to emphasise that the consumer may have been totally or partially unaware of the problem before viewing the advertising material. Did this problem already exist but had not been formally identified? Or, was this problem created, perhaps in part, by advertising discourse itself? To return to Talbot's (2010a: 40) example in Chapter 2 of adverts asking their addressee: 'are you doing enough for your underarms?', the underarm may be created as a problematic body part that requires specialised solutions in the form of particular products.

After the potential Problems (with the three key ones outlined above), the model continues with the Response (Solution). As in the original model, this can take the form of a Positive Evaluation, a Positive Result, or a Positive Result/Evaluation combined. The addition to the Response in the adapted model is that all Response elements can optionally include Surface Appearance discourse (skin **looks** smoother; fine lines **appear** reduced) and/ or Transformation discourse (**transforms** your skin; a moisture **revolution**), and/or Fragmentation of body parts (leaves **your hair** beautifully soft). These are three common features of female media discourse outlined by Benwell and Stokoe (2006), but they have not previously been connected specifically to Hoey's pattern. Fragmentation in the Response tends to connect with Problem 1: Fragmented Aspect of Appearance. The process of Fragmentation in female-targeted texts may serve to identify women primarily in terms of their (problematic) body parts (Mills 1995: 171–172; Byerly and Ross 2006; Benwell and Stokoe 2006: 172; Jeffries 2007: 71; Talbot 2010b: 133). In addition, this phenomenon facilitates a process of consumption through the body, with specially targeted products being advertised to the consumer (Benwell and Stokoe 2006: 172). In the data analysed, two main manifestations of Fragmentation are evident: visual Fragmentation through close-up shots or particular camera angles drawing attention to various body parts; and textual Fragmentation through use of lexical items denoting (greasy) **hair**, (dull) **skin**, (brittle) **nails**, and so on.

The second kind of discourse found in the Response elements is a Transformation discourse in which the female consumer is encouraged to change her appearance in some way through purchase and usage of the products advertised (Benwell and Stokoe 2006: 176). In this way, transformation more generally can be regarded as '[…] the lifeblood of consumerism since it relies on other consumer products or objects for its facilitation', and discursively this is often produced through use of the product name combined with verbs such as **improve**, **reduce**, or **reveal** (Benwell and Stokoe 2006: 176). This transformation of self through use of a particular cosmetic may be presented as going beyond the outer body and even producing a change in 'inner' self or identity, in that improvements to one's appearance can help women to feel more positive, confident, and so on, with the suggestion that this could translate to other aspects of their lives (Benwell and Stokoe 2006: 176).

A discourse of Surface Appearance can also be identified in texts of Consumer/Commodified Femininity and this is often realised through the verb **look** or the adjective **looking** (Benwell and Stokoe 2006: 176). Oft-cited examples from beauty advertising are **fine lines and wrinkles appear reduced** or **skin looks smoother**. This use of 'mitigatory elements' could mean that fine lines and wrinkles are not actually reduced: they only *appear* to be so (Coupland 2003: 139–140). Skin may look smoother, but it is not actually smoother. As mentioned in Chapter 1, this distinction is in part a legal one and to do with adherence to the regulatory bodies regarding misleading claims.[7] If a cosmetic *does* alter skin's function then it could fit into the category of a drug, which demands a different kind of licensing and regulation from cosmetics. However, 'reduces the appearance of' may lead some consumers to believe that fine lines and wrinkles are themselves reduced (Benwell and Stokoe 2006: 178). Additionally, the lack of permanency to the Solutions provided will hopefully (from the perspective of the brand) lead to repeat purchases in order to attain repeat/continued product effects. The following section applies the adapted model to selected examples, exploring the different stages.

APPLYING THE ADAPTED PROBLEM-SOLUTION MODEL

Figure 3.3 represents the application of this new model to *Aussie* Lusciously Light 3 Minute Miracle deep conditioner (*Elle* UK May 2011), in which the pattern begins with a variety of what we might call 'life' Problems (Problem 3: Lifestyle or Environment):

Bulging handbags. Mobile phones. Emotional baggage.

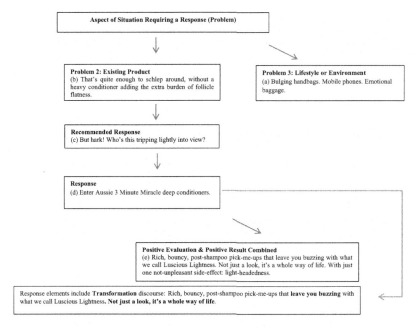

Fig. 3.3 Worked example of *Aussie* Lusciously Light 3 Minute Miracle deep conditioner

The next lines set up an additional problem as Problem 2: Existing Product, which is in this case heavy conditioner:

> That's quite enough to schlep around, without a heavy conditioner adding the extra burden of follicle flatness.

Thus, **heavy** is constructed as semantically negative when it is modifying **conditioner**. The negative connotations are intensified by **extra burden** and the alliterative **follicle flatness**. This example then contains an intermediate stage that we could classify as a Recommended Response, in which the product is personified as some kind of 'hair saviour', with **lightly** in contrast to the **heavy** conditioner:

> But hark! Who's this tripping lightly into view?

We then have the Response proper:

> Enter Aussie 3 Minute Miracle deep conditioners

and the product is then introduced further with a combined Positive Result and Positive Evaluation:

> Rich, bouncy, post-shampoo-pick-me-ups that leave you buzzing with what we call Luscious Lightness. Not just a look, it's a whole way of life. With just one not-unpleasant side-effect: light-headedness.

The lexical items **rich, bouncy, lightness**, and **pick-me-ups** reinforce the idea of lightness and a sense of revival for the hair. The pun **light-headedness** also works in this way, contrasting with the **heavy** conditioners already on the market. Transformation discourse is also at work here, suggesting (perhaps in a tongue-in-cheek manner) that this product is life-changing.

Figure 3.4 shows the application of the adapted Problem-Solution pattern to *Neutrogena* Multi-Defence Daily Moisturiser (*Cosmopolitan* May UK 2011). Again, this example involves more than one Problem. It begins with an implied Problem, which is the failing of other existing (and possibly inferior) products (Problem 2: Existing Product):

> Go beyond moisture.

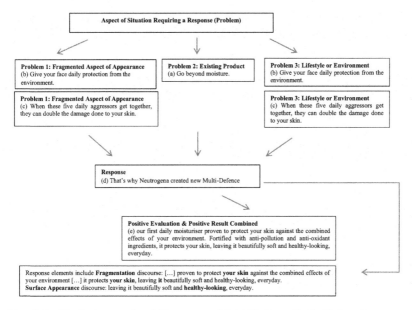

Fig. 3.4   Worked example of *Neutrogena* Multi-Defence Daily Moisturiser

This implies that other products simply moisturise, whereas this product does something more, which will be elaborated on in the continuing text of the advertisement. Fragmentation of body parts presents the face as something in need of protection (Problem 1: Fragmented Aspect of Appearance, Problem 3: Lifestyle or Environment), and the negative effects of the environment can apparently be offset by use of this particular product:

Give your face daily protection from the environment.

The environment in this case is lexically constructed as having negative connotations through a discourse of protection against its effects. The product is then introduced through **new** and **Multi-Defence Daily Moisturiser**, with **defence** adding to the discourse of protection. The image in this particular example is important in constructing the Problem-Solution pattern. The product itself is reproduced in the advertisement as a bottle of moisturiser with a ring around it like a shield, and on the outside of the shield are the negative parts of the environment that require protecting against: wind, heat, pollution, sun, and cold. This creates quite a striking visual metaphor, which is then emphasised in the following continuation of the problem. The vocabulary of attack is highlighted below, corresponding to Lazar's (2006) analysis of Singaporean cosmetics advertising in which women are warned they should be **fighting** against negative effects on their skin:

> When these five daily **aggressors** get together, they can double the **damage** done to your skin.

The Response is lexically signalled by **that's why**, a prototypical but perhaps now slightly outdated feature of advertising discourse. The Problem is re-emphasised after the Solution is introduced, with Fragmentation of the addressee's skin:

> That's why Neutrogena created new Multi-Defence, our first daily moisturiser proven to protect your skin against the combined effects of your environment.

The advertisement ends with a combined Positive Result and Positive Evaluation, again drawing on the discourse of protection:

> fortified with anti-pollution and anti-oxidant ingredients, it protects your skin, leaving it beautifully soft and healthy-looking, everyday.

This Positive Result/Positive Evaluation has another instance of Fragmentation. It also uses a discourse of Surface Appearance in the adjectival phrase **healthy-looking**. Skin may not actually *be* healthy, but appears so.

Figure 3.5 shows the application of the model to *Clarins* Multi-Active Jour [Multi-Active day cream] from *Elle* France 6 May 2011. This example begins with the Problem, which involves two of the three Problems from the adapted model: firstly, with a fragmented aspect of ageing on the face (Problem 1: Fragmented Aspect of Appearance):

> Rides précoces? Non merci! [Early wrinkles? No thank you!][8]

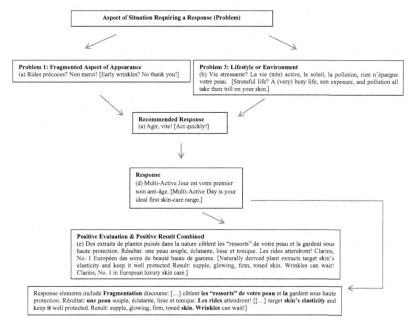

Fig. 3.5 Worked example of *Clarins* Multi-Active Jour [Multi-Active day cream]

The second is in fact a range of problems with modern life and physical environment (Problem 3: Lifestyle or Environment):

> Vie stressante? La vie (très) active, le soleil, la pollution, rien n'épargne votre peau. [Stressful life? A (very) busy life, sun exposure, and pollution all take their toll on your skin.]

After outlining the Problem, the Recommended Response is signalled by a call to action on the part of the reader/addressee in the form of an imperative:

> Agir, vite! [Act quickly!]

The product itself, an anti-ageing skin cream, is presented as the positive antidote (Response) to these issues. In the next section of the advert we have a Positive Response and a recasting of the Problem with

Fragmentation of the skin. In connection with Problem 3 (Lifestyle or Environment), we again come across a discourse of protecting your skin (Lazar 2006) from the range of stressors mentioned above:

> Multi-Active Jour est votre premier soin anti-âge. Des extraits de plantes puisés dans la nature ciblent les "ressorts" de votre peau et la gardent sous haute protection. [Multi-Active Day is your ideal first skincare range. Naturally derived plant extracts target skin's elasticity and keep it well protected.]

This example ends with combined Positive Evaluation and Positive Responses, with the advertisement even using the noun 'Résultat' [Result], and Fragmentation being used to emphasise the product effects:

> Résultat: une peau souple, éclatante, lisse et tonique. Les rides attendront! Clarins, No. 1 Européen des soins de beauté haute de gamme. [Result: supple, glowing, firm, toned skin. Wrinkles can wait! Clarins, No. 1 in European luxury skincare.]

In *Max Factor* False Lash Effect Fusion Mascara from *Elle* UK June 2011 (Fig. 3.6), the pattern begins with the Response, which is also a summary of the gist of the Problem-Solution pattern in this particular example:

> New False Lash Effect Fusion Mascara. Volume and Length. Get it together.

The remaining text in the advertisement addresses the Problem of an existing product (Problem 2: Existing Product) not fulfilling the required needs (in this example we have a testimonial from a make-up artist in the advertisement). The issue in the past was apparently that in fact *two* products were needed in order to attain the desired effect: a volume and a strengthening mascara were needed for **incredible lashes**.

> Models need incredible lashes, and until now I've used a volume and strengthening mascara.

Max Factor have apparently solved this problem through the product advertised, and the beginning of the Response is signalled by **not any more**. This is continued in the combined Positive Result/Positive Evaluation:

> Max Factor have fused their MEGA VOLUMISING BRUSH with their ULTIMATE LENGTHENING FORMULA for 100% lash glamour.

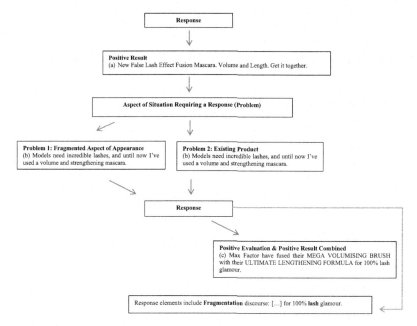

Fig. 3.6 Worked example of *Max Factor* False Lash Effect Fusion Mascara

Eucerin AQUAporin Active moisturising cream (*Elle* UK May 2011) (Fig. 3.7) begins with a suggestion that other products are inferior in their moisturising capabilities (Problem 2: Existing Product):

Instead of simply locking moisture into your skin...

This presupposes that some products just lock moisture into one's skin, but that this product goes far beyond this. The personal pronoun employed in **your skin** is an example of Fragmentation here, and the direct address may aim to create some kind of relationship with the target female (this is discussed later in the chapter). The next part continues as a Positive Response with further fragmentation of the body part **your skin**:

We've explored ways of helping your skin distribute moisture more effectively.

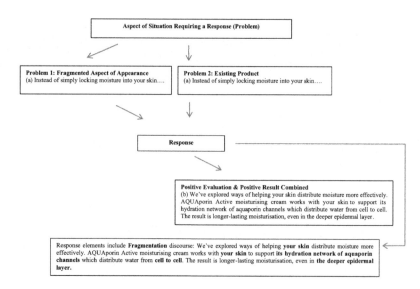

Fig. 3.7   Worked example of *Eucerin* AQUAporin Active moisturising cream

The verb **helping** with the adverbial phrase **more effectively** signals a Positive Result here. As the advertisement continues, further explanation is needed because of the scientific-sounding register. The addressee might not know what **aquaporin channels** are:

> AQUAporin Active moisturising cream works with your skin to support its hydration network of aquaporin channels which distribute water from cell to cell.

The Result is then lexically signalled as such, with a combined Positive Result/Evaluation:

> The result is longer-lasting moisturisation, even in the deeper epidermal layer.

There are several Fragmentation examples in the Response, emphasising the effects that this product has on skin: **your skin**; **its hydration network of aquaporin channels**; **cell to cell**; **in the deeper epidermal layer**.

As mentioned previously, this kind of Fragmentation is common within the Problem-Solution pattern, often taking the form of lexical items denoting body parts. The second person pronoun **your** often precedes these body parts:

Instead of simply locking moisture into **your skin**, we've explored ways of helping **your skin** distribute moisture more effectively (*Eucerin* AQUAporin Active moisturising cream, *Elle* UK July 2011)

So effective, **your skin** looks purer and more radiant (*Vichy* Normaderm Tri-Activ Anti-Imperfection Hydrating Care, *Cosmopolitan* May UK 2011)

Enriched with Vitamin B3 and natural oils, it noticeably improves **your skin** in 3 weeks (*E45* DermaRestore Endless Moisture body lotion, *Elle* UK June 2011)

The new VO5 shampoo and conditioner range has Adaptive Haircare Technology which adjusts to provide the right level of nourishment **your hair** needs, where it needs it (*VO5* haircare range, *Elle* UK August 2011)

The Pantene Pro-V conditioning formulas help protect **your colour** for up to 8 weeks (*Pantene* Pro-V Colour Protect and Smooth collection hair shampoos and conditioners, *Elle* UK July 2011)

Efficacité prouvée sur **le visage, les mains,** et **le décolleté** [Proven effective on **face, hands,** and **décolletage**] (*Clinique* Even Better Concentré Anti-Taches Correction Teint [dark spot corrector], *Elle* France 2 September 2011)

La recette pour démêler et réparer jusqu'aux pointes **les cheveux longs**

The recipe for detangling and repairing **long hair** right to the tips (*Garnier* Ultra Doux au lait de vanille et pulpe de papaye [vanilla and papaya pulp shampoo], *Elle* France 30 September 2011)

Vos rides sont visiblement réduites en 4 semaines, **votre peau** paraît plus jeune [**Your wrinkles** are visibly reduced in 4 weeks, **your skin** appears younger] (*Nivea* Pure and Natural soin de jour anti-rides [anti-wrinkle day cream], *Elle* France 22 July 2011)

Clinically proven to improve all of **5 winter skin symptoms: dry, tight, sensitive, rough, uncomfortable** (*Aveeno* Skin Relief lotion, *Cosmopolitan* May UK 2011)

The first fast-acting serum from Estée Lauder Research to significantly reduce the look of **blotchiness, past blemish marks** and **discolourations** (*Estée Lauder* Idéalist Serum, *Elle* UK July 2011)

La lotion clarifiante balaie **les cellules mortes** pour **une peau saine, éclatante, idéalement préparée pour l'été** [The clarifying lotion lifts off **dead skin cells for healthy, glowing skin, perfectly ready for summer**] (*Clinique* Le Basic 3 Temps [3 Step Skincare], *Elle* France 15 July 2011).

The use of synthetic personalisation or direct address (Fairclough 2015: 89; see also Talbot 1995) is evident in the use of **your skin, hair, colour**, and so on, with the French using the more formal second person pronoun **votre**. The use of **your/votre** may be a deliberate technique to create the impression that the product is specifically tailored for the target consumer. The body parts are often preceded by an adjective such as dry (skin) or coloured (hair): these describe both the current state of the body part with the potential for improvement or special treatment (for example, dry hair needs moisture; coloured hair needs a tailored product).

Some of the Fragmentation examples work on a visual level. In *Garnier* Pure-Active spot concealer (*Elle* UK May 2011), the facial blemish is construed as a target, creating the impression that the Solution to the product is specialised, with connotations of precise application. The Fragmentation of the spot is the offending aspect of appearance (Problem 1: Fragmented Aspect of Appearance) and this is identified through use of the target. In other advertisements such as *L'Oréal* Youth

Code face cream (*Elle* UK June 2011), various facial parts are identified via lines and bullet points. This implies these face areas might be problematic, and it also suggests that the product can help to 'solve' or improve these areas of the face. The visual here has links to precision and works well with the scientific register elsewhere in the advertisement. The close-up image adds to the sense of an effective product, which suggests visible results can be attained.

Another element of Solution is that of Transformation discourse, which uses lexical items to connote a feeling of offering a full, positive Response. The lexical markers of Transformation discourse, such as **transform**, **reduce**, and **reveal**, are highlighted in bold in the following examples:

The first fast-acting serum from Estée Lauder Research to **significantly reduce** the look of blotchiness, past blemish marks and discolorations (*Estée Lauder* Idéalist Even Skintone Illuminator, *Cosmopolitan* UK July 2011)

Rich, creamy and luxurious Palmer's Cocoa Butter Formula helps **transform** the roughest, driest skin into soft and beautiful (*Palmer's* Cocoa Butter Formula body moisturiser, *Cosmopolitan* UK June 2011)

Le 1er sérum action rapide de la recherche Estée Lauder pour **estomper visiblement** rougeurs, taches de soleil et taches brunes (*Estée Lauder* Idéalist sérum correcteur de teint unifiant illuminateur [see first example for official translation], *Elle* France 23 September 2011)

Le savon visage **élimine** les impuretés pour une peau saine [Facial soap **eliminates** impurities for healthy skin] (*Clinique* Le Basic 3 Temps [3 Step Skincare], *Cosmopolitan* France August 2011)

Clarins Daily Energizers are packed with natural extracts to **help diminish** imperfections and to **energise** and **boost** skin's radiance (*Clarins* Daily Energizer Cream-Gel, *Elle* UK August 2011)

Reduces wrinkle appearance in 28 days guaranteed or your money back (*Olay* Professional skincare ranges, *Elle* UK September 2011)

Improves shine 35% (*Paul Mitchell* Awapuhi hair care, *Elle* UK July 2011)

Also featuring in some of the Solutions was Surface Appearance discourse. In the following examples, the lexical items in bold highlight the careful wording used to describe the product effects. Notably, the product effects emphasise how the female consumer's body, skin, or hair *looks* or *feels* better in some way post-product usage:

> So, if you are not looking for a permanent lift, Liftactiv Derm Source **reduces the appearance of** wrinkles and leaves skin **feeling firmer** (*Vichy* Liftactiv Derm Source anti-wrinkle and firming moisturiser, *Elle* UK June 2011)

> Skin that **looks younger, smoother and brighter** (*L'Oréal* Paris Youth Code cream and serum, *Cosmopolitan* UK June 2011)

> Skin **feels** lusciously fresh and **looks gorgeously flawless** (*Clarins* HydraQuench Tinted Moisturiser, *Cosmopolitan* UK July 2011)

> **Covers** dark circles and fine lines to **help conceal** crow's feet—**as if erased**! (*Maybelline* The Eraser Perfect and Cover foundation, *Elle* UK May 2011)

> Discover our perfect combination: serum + day cream for skin that **looks rejuvenated and brighter** (*L'Oréal* Youth Code Cream and Serum, *Elle* UK May 2011)

> Optics downsize **the appearance** of pores while our Pore Resurfacing Complex quickly, gently clears out debris and rough flakes (*Clinique* Pore Refining Solutions Correcting Serum, *Elle* UK September 2011)

> Vos rides sont **visiblement réduites** en 4 semaines, votre peau **paraît** plus jeune [Your wrinkles are **visibly reduced** in 4 weeks, your skin **appears** younger] (*Nivea* Pure and Natural soin de jour anti-rides [anti-wrinkle day cream], *Elle* France 22 July 2011)

> L'intensité des cernes est **visiblement réduite** [The depth of dark circles is **visibly reduced**] (*Garnier* roll-on anti-cernes [anti-dark circles roll-on], *Cosmopolitan* France May 2011)

So effective, your skin **looks** purer and more radiant (*Vichy* Normaderm Tri-Activ Anti-Imperfection Hydrating Care, *Cosmopolitan* May UK 2011)

1. Dark circles **appear** reduced. 2 Bags **appear** reduced. 3. Eye contour **looks** more luminous. 4. Eye contour **looks** smoother. 5. Eye contour **feels** firmer. 6. The skin around the eye area **appears** smoother (*Lancôme* Multiple Lift eye cream, *Elle* UK June 2011)

The selected examples above are typical of this kind of discourse, in which the language of Surface Appearance was often used in conjunction with product effects on the relevant body part.

French-English Comparisons

The Problem-Solution pattern was found to be a common occurrence in the advertisements analysed: out of 495 advertisements, 328 contained the Problem-Solution pattern (66 %). If we consider how the French and English data differed, 180 out of 249 French advertisements displayed the Problem-Solution pattern (72 %) compared with 148 out of 246 English advertisements (60 %). A chi-square test was conducted using SPSS in order to see whether this difference was statistically significant. The null hypothesis would predict that the difference between the frequency of the Problem-Solution pattern in the French data and the English data under analysis could have occurred by chance. The alternative hypothesis is that the difference between the frequency of the Problem-Solution pattern in the French data and the English data under analysis is not simply due to chance. The chi-square test produced a p value equal to 0.004. As p is less than 0.05 (5 %), we have sufficient evidence to reject the null hypothesis, suggesting that the difference is statistically significant.

If we consider why this might be the case, the higher level of Problem-Solution patterning may be linked to the increased frequency of scientific-sounding language in the French data analysed. This phenomenon is explored in more detail in Chapter 5.[9] As French adverts tend to prefer a more scientific register, the Problem-Solution pattern may add to this discourse by appearing (re)assuring for the consumer and presenting the argument of the advertisement in a systematic, formulaic way. The Responses offered tend to include scientific-sounding ingredients to address a certain Problem, with the Basis providing an opportunity for the brand to discuss clinical trials, tests on female consumers, and so on. In this way, a scientific register fits comfortably within the Problem-Solution pattern in terms of providing evidence and authenticity.

As emphasised throughout this chapter, the improvements offered in the Solution elements can only affect skin's appearance or surface. As such, they are not permanent but rather a temporary fix or disguise, which supports Benwell and Stokoe's (2006: 176) argument that the problems of Consumer/Commodified Femininity can never really be solved. In addition, the analysis demonstrated a connection between the Problem and a negative portrayal of ageing, which requires various Solutions. This finding corresponds with previous literature on the construction of ageing in female-targeted media discourse as something that must be striven against at all costs through purchase and usage of beauty products and, in more extreme cases, surgical interventions (Wolf 1991; Coupland 2003, 2007; Benwell and Stokoe 2006). In cosmetics advertising discourse, the emphasis is on the consumer to recognise the problems constructed in the advertisement, match these up with her own problems, and then take the necessary remedial action. In doing so, these kinds of advertisements may invoke a discourse of empowerment and self-improvement in which choice is key, without perhaps interrogating the societal constraints and gendered norms surrounding these kinds of choices (Lazar 2006; Gill 2007a, 2007b, 2009; McRobbie 2009; Orbach 2010: 91).

NOTES

1. Many female-targeted magazines have begun running features on 'body positivity' and the importance of accepting one's flaws, in the midst of advertorials and advertisements suggesting ways to improve one's appearance.
2. Helen Mirren's recent role in a *L'Oréal* UK skincare advertisement would be one exception, although the narrative does suggest that women always want to appear much younger, and perhaps healthier, than they actually are and that products can be a useful tool in this fight against visual identifiers of ageing.

3. Gauntlett (2008: 88) wryly notes that although men are under some pressure to look a certain way, their personalities can be redeeming in a way women's cannot: 'Men are ideally required to be thin and well-toned too, but can get away with imperfections as long as they can compensate with charm or humour'.

4. Rhode (2010: 7) succinctly argues: 'Women face greater pressures than men to look attractive and pay greater penalties for falling short'.

5. This gives rise to the so-called 'silver foxes' such as Hollywood actor George Clooney.

6. Not all examples fit neatly into this distinction. Bednarek (2009) for example suggests the need to look more closely at both the type of attitudinal lexis involved *and* the type of attitudinal target or assessment.

7. See for example 'ASA Hot Topic: Health and beauty': https://www.asa.org. uk/News-resources/Hot-Topics/Health-and-beauty.aspx#.VsGkHfl4a70

8. All advertisement translations throughout the book are my own, except where identical English and French versions appeared in the dataset. In those cases, the 'official' translation is used and signalled as such.

9. See also Ringrow (2014).

REFERENCES

Bednarek, M. (2009). Language patterns and attitude. *Functions of Language, 16*(2), 165–192.

Benwell, B., & Stokoe, E. (2006). *Discourse and identity*. Edinburgh: Edinburgh University Press.

Byerly, C., & Ross, K. (2006). *Women and media: A critical introduction*. Oxford: Blackwell.

Chivers, S. (2003). *From old women to older women: Contemporary culture and women's narratives*. Columbus: Ohio State University Press.

Coupland, J. (2003). Ageist ideology and discourses of control in skincare product marketing. In J. Coupland & R. Gwyn (Eds.), *Discourse, the body and identity* (pp. 127–150). Basingstoke: Palgrave Macmillan.

Coupland, J. (2007). Gendered discourses on the 'problem' of ageing: Consumerised solutions. *Discourse and Communication, 1*(1), 37–61.

Fairclough, N. (2015). *Language and power* (3rd ed.). Harlow: Longman.

Gauntlett, D. (2008). *Media, gender and identity: An introduction* (2nd ed.). London: Routledge.

Gill, R. (2007a). *Gender and the media*. Cambridge: Cambridge University Press.

Gill, R. (2007b). Postfeminist media culture: Elements of a sensibility. *European Journal of Cultural Studies, 10*(2), 147–166.

Gill, R. (2009). Supersexualize me! Advertising, (post) feminism and "the midriffs". In F. Attwood (Ed.), *Mainstreaming sex: The sexualisation of Western culture*. New York: IB Tauris.

Harrison, C. (2008). Real men do wear mascara: Advertising discourse and masculine identity. *Critical Discourse Studies, 5*(1), 55–73.

Harrison, C. (2012). Studio5ive.com: Selling cosmetics to men and reconstructing masculine identity. In K. Ross (Ed.), *The handbook of gender, sex and media* (pp. 189–204). London: Wiley-Blackwell.

Hoey, M. (1983). *On the surface of discourse*. London: Allen and Unwin.

Hoey, M. (2001). *Textual interaction: An introduction to written discourse analysis*. London: Routledge.

Hurd Clarke, L. (2011). *Facing age: Women growing older in anti-aging culture*. Plymouth: Rowman and Littlefield.

Jeffries, L. (2007). *The textual construction of the female body: A critical discourse analysis approach*. Basingstoke: Palgrave Macmillan.

Lazar, M. (2006). "Discover the power of femininity!" Analysing global "power femininity" in local advertising. *Feminist Media Studies: New Femininities, 6*(4), 505–517.

Martin, J., & White, P. (2005). *The language of evaluation: Appraisal in English*. Basingstoke: Palgrave Macmillan.

McRobbie, A. (2009). *The aftermath of feminism: Gender, culture and social change*. London: SAGE.

Mills, S. (1995). *Feminist stylistics*. London: Routledge.

Nelson, J. (2012). *Airbrushed nation*. Berkeley: Seal Press.

Orbach, S. (2010). *Bodies*. London: Profile.

Rhode, D. (2010). *The beauty bias: The injustice of appearance in life and law*. New York: Oxford University Press.

Ringrow, H. (2014). Peptides, proteins and peeling active ingredients: Exploring 'scientific' language in English and French cosmetics advertising. *Études de Stylistique Anglaise, 7*, 183–210.

Simpson, P., & Mayr, A. (2010). *Language and power*. London: Routledge.

Sontag, S. (1972). The double standard of ageing. *The Saturday Review*, pp. 29–38.

Talbot, M. (1995). A synthetic sisterhood: False friends in a teenage magazine. In M. Bucholtz & K. Hall (Eds.), *Gender articulated: Language and the socially constructed self* (pp. 143–168). London: Routledge.

Talbot, M. (2010a). *Language and gender* (2nd ed.). Cambridge: Polity Press.

Talbot, M. (2010b). *Language, intertextuality and subjectivity: Voices in the construction of consumer femininity*. Saarbrücken: Lambert Academic Publishing.

Wolf, N. (1991). *The beauty myth: How images of beauty are used against women.* London: Vintage.

Woodward, K. (1991). *Aging and its discontents: Freud and other fictions.* Bloomington/Indianapolis: Indiana University Press.

Wykes, M., & Gunter, B. (2005). *The media and body image: If looks could kill.* London: SAGE.

CHAPTER 4

Femininity as a Sensual Identity

Abstract This chapter examines how cosmetics advertisements connect femininity to sensuality. Key debates surrounding sensual and/or sexual representations of the female body in media discourse are addressed. The chapter moves on to explore sensual discourse that describes cosmetic products' qualities, actions, and effects, in addition to visual signifiers of sensuality such as parted lips, nudity, and the use of sensory modality in product images. The chapter compares and contrasts sensual advertising discourse in English and French contexts, with a particular emphasis on nudity across cultures.

Keywords Sensuality in the media • Cosmetics advertisements • Advertising across cultures • Sensory modality • Nudity across cultures

LANGUAGE, SENSUALITY, AND THE FEMALE BODY

This chapter explores how cosmetics advertisements connect femininity to sensuality. This occurs in two main ways. Firstly, the sensory effects of cosmetics are highlighted using a 'subjective, affective language' that 'links even the most unlikely products to *sensation* or *sensuality*' (Benwell and Stokoe 2006: 173, original emphasis). Conditioner *envelops* hair; face creams feel *luxurious*, skin is left *supple* and *beautified*; lips are *caressed*. In more extreme cases, products are even shown to be giving some kind of sexual pleasure to the female model in the advertisement (Penny 2011: 9). Secondly, the usage of young, prototypically 'sexy' women in the advertisements associates the product with female sensuality. Arguably, the advertisements' associations with sensuality can be placed within the wider context of the magazine publications in which they appear. Women's glossy magazines, with *Cosmopolitan* perhaps being the obvious example, often contain highly sexual content, including (heterosexual) sexual techniques, tips, and positions (Gauntlett 2008: 198–199). The sensualisation of advertising and magazine content is therefore of mutual economic benefit to cosmetics brands and magazine publishers, which will be discussed more fully later in this chapter.

It may be useful at this stage to explore issues of terminology. Arguably, the kind of language explored in this chapter is more of a *sensual* discourse as opposed to an explicitly *sexual* one. The focus in cosmetics advertisements tends to be on the product's pleasurable effects on women's skin, hair, and so on. In practice, it can sometimes be difficult to distinguish between *sensual* and *sexual* and there is certainly a degree of subjectivity in the interpretation. For example, in much UK media, any appearance of female nudity is generally seen as sexualised. However, as discussed later, whether nudity is *always* sexual in this context is open to some debate.

With this in mind, the sexual and/or sensual representation of the female body in media contexts (and in relation to societal, cultural, and religious norms) is something that has attracted much attention from linguists and non-linguists alike. Second-wave feminist texts that have considered the representation of women's bodies in popular culture include, notably, Greer's *The Female Eunuch* (1971) and de Beauvoir's The Second Sex (1949, original French edition). More recent feminist treatments of female sexual (mis)representation in media discourse include Wolf's *The Beauty Myth* (1991), Penny's *Meat Market: Female Flesh Under Capitalism* (2011), and Walter's *Living Dolls* (2010). Vehement criticism of nudity and sexualised content in media discourse has often come from groups holding disparate views, such as the conservative 'religious right' (who express concerns about an apparently sex-saturated, morally corrupt society) and feminist organisations (who argue against the sexual objectification of women by men). Despite some sense of backlash against overtly sexual media content (such as the recent *No More Page 3* campaign[1]), sex, in varying forms and to various degrees, continues to be ubiquitous in advertising.

In particular, the increased sexualisation of young girls in Western culture is a topic that has attracted much attention. Levy (2006), Walter (2010), Banyard (2011), Durham (2009), Orenstein (2011), and others all address the issue of what they regard as an oversexualised media culture, which may be detrimental to girls' social, sexual, educational, and psychological development. Manifestations of this culture include young girls idolising the sexualised *Bratz* dolls, wearing thongs with *sexy* emblazoned on the front, and watching female pop stars on the television wearing very little clothing while gyrating to music with sexually explicit lyrics. Durham terms this 'the Lolita effect': 'the distorted and delusional set of myths about girls' sexuality that circulates widely in our culture and throughout the world, that works to limit, undermine, and restrict girls' sexual progress' (2009: 12). As young girls approach adulthood and begin to engage with media targeted at older females, the femininities on offer may further reinforce those childhood models (Walter 2010: 2). At times, the media models of femininity for young girls may even appear similar to the ideals of femininity presented in soft pornography (Durham 2009: 66), although how pornography differs from non-pornographic contemporary Western media visuals is often not entirely clear (Waters 2007: 251–252). Some scholars attribute this media sexualisation of younger children to the infiltration of the porn industry and related elements into mainstream Western media and culture, and into advertising in particular (Wolf 1991; McNair 2002; Levy 2006; Attwood 2009; Gill 2009; Walter 2010). In most advertising contexts, female nudity is still more prevalent than male nudity (although this may be increasing somewhat) (Gill 2007: 104; Gauntlett 2008: 196; Durham 2009: 167). The argument that women's bodies are inherently more attractive or erotic than men's is not entirely plausible, especially given that the ideal female body has changed dramatically according to time and culture (Wolf 1991: 12–13; Durham 2009: 77; Banyard 2011: 8–20).

Scholars within childhood education are somewhat critical of the furore surrounding the oversexualisation of children in contemporary media (see for example Buckingham and Bragg 2004; Buckingham 2011). As alluded to earlier in this chapter, there is some debate about the terms 'sexual' and 'sexualised', which are not universally agreed-upon concepts. In most of the literature on this topic, 'sexualised' tends to be equated with 'objectification', which might not always be the case (Buckingham 2011: 128–131). Similarly, what is deemed 'appropriate' for children versus adults is also up for discussion. Use of nudity may not always be inappropriate or sexualised, although what a nude, non-sexualised body in advertising might actually look like poses some interesting questions (Buckingham 2011: 137). A major concern for many education scholars is the lack of research that takes into account children's perspectives on this subject matter. Research that *has* explored children's responses to sexual or sensual advertising materials suggests that older children tend to be more critical than the media moral panic gives them credit for, whilst younger children may often be unaware of sexual innuendo or content (see for example Buckingham and Bragg 2004).

In the debate about sexualisation of media content, discussions surrounding the representations of the female body in advertising are particularly relevant to this chapter. In advertising material, the sexual female body is linked to media standards of beauty and femininity.[2] The overall media message can often be summarised as '[...] if you're female, your desirability is contingent on blatant bodily display' (Durham 2009: 77). Furthermore, bodies are encouraged to conform to various standards through discipline and product use (Walter 2010: 3). This is a view shared by Gill (2009: 100), who argues that '[...] instead of caring or nurturing or motherhood, it is the possession of a "sexy body" that is presented as women's key source of identity'.[3] The representation of female sexual identity in the media could, in theory, be a positive sign of female empowerment. Gill (2009: 94) has argued that in the media since 1994, women's bodies have been displayed less as sexually passive and more as pleasure-seeking. Gill cites the example of Eva Herzigova's *Wonderbra* advertisements ('Hello boys'; 'Or are you just pleased to see me?') to show how women are depicted as active sexual participants with their own physical needs and desires, although often with a somewhat ironic and/or playful tone in these kinds of advertisements (Gill 2009: 97, 2007: 89–90). This consideration of female sexuality forms part of what Gill (2009) terms Midriff Advertising, aimed at young women with an interest in fashion. These women are less likely to respond well to representations of females as passive sex objects as this may contradict their own experiences. An emphasis on an apparently empowered female sexuality may to some extent be an attempt to cater to this demographic (Gill 2009: 99).[4] In this way, these kinds of advertising representations can be linked to Goldman's (1992) Commodity Feminism and Lazar's (2006) Power Femininity, in which a sexy body may be portrayed in the media as bringing the female consumer some kind of power: material, sexual, or otherwise, although in reality this could be far from the case (see Gill 2009: 100).

As Gill (2009: 104, original emphasis) argues: '[...] midriff advertising *re-sexualises* women's bodies, with the excuse of a feisty, empowered post-feminist discourse that makes it very difficult to critique'. Added to this is the idea of a new 'self-policing narcissistic gaze' in addition to (and perhaps overtaking) the traditional male gaze, thus women may be presented in media as both object and subject: 'not only are women objectified as they were before, but through sexual subjectification they must also understand their own objectification as pleasurable and self-chosen' (Gill 2009: 107). Any discussion of positive female empowerment through sexual advertising discourse should therefore be approached with some caution. While it could be positive that women are portrayed as having sexual desires, the limiting sexual identity that is often equated with this type of advertising discourse may have a negative impact on women's self-esteem or even their own personal sexual experiences.

In addition to the work of Benwell and Stokoe (2006) mentioned at the start of this chapter, a range of linguistic research has explored how the female body is constructed in a sensualised or sexualised manner, particularly in a media context. Machin and Thornborrow (2003) focus mainly on the discourse of *Cosmopolitan* magazine *content*, as opposed to the advertising; however, their work provides a useful context to assess the environment in which sensualised cosmetics advertisements appear. Images in *Cosmopolitan* generally depict women in abstract settings and in overtly sexualised ways: red lipstick, long hair, revealing clothing, high heels (Machin and Thornborrow 2003: 458–461). In their multimodal analysis, Machin and Thornborrow (2003: 460) argue that '[...] female agency is linked to sexuality and the body, whether work, love and/or sexual relationships are represented'. Regarding the written articles, there is a strong emphasis on heterosexual sex, in particular on how to *feel* and *appear* sexually confident (Machin and Thornborrow 2003: 462–465). Similarly, Jeffries (2007) examines the way in which women's magazine discourse represents the female body, particularly how readers are often made to feel that their body does not quite reach the required standard. In turn, this can be linked to sexuality, as many of the magazine articles focus on how the reader can achieve beauty, and therefore, both implicitly and explicitly, sexual attractiveness (2007: 100–101). To achieve **come-to-bed hair**, for example, readers are advised to **first give their hair a lift** using a particular product, and Jeffries argues that examples like these '[...] demonstrate the direct link between beauty and its ideological aim, which is to have sex' (Jeffries 2007: 101). Appearance and sexual behaviour therefore tend to be linked in media female representations. Mills (1995) has also addressed the portrayal of the female body in a range of domains, with an emphasis on advertising texts and images. She draws attention to the use of (semi-) nude women and a discourse of female sexuality to sell a wide range of products, arguing that 'women's defining feature' is seen as being 'sexual and sexually available' (Mills 1995: 176–178). The following sections will explore English and French examples of sensual discourse commonly found in contemporary cosmetics advertising. As such, the discussion aims to build upon the observations of Benwell and Stokoe (2006) that subjective, affective language in cosmetics advertising discourse connects the product to sensuality.

Sensual Lexis: Product Qualities

Contemporary cosmetics advertisements tend to be described using adjectives or adverbs connoting sensuality. *Lancôme* L'Absolu Nu lipstick (*Elle* UK May 2011) describes the various shades of the product as '**sexy** nudes' which are '**provocatively** radiant' and '**irresistibly** lightweight'. An advertisement for *Guerlain* Rouge lipstick (*Elle* France 6 May 2011) contains the description 'rouge **irresistible** automatiquement' [automatically **irresistible** [irresistible] red lipstick]. Similarly, *Maybelline* GlamShine Fresh lipgloss (*Elle* France 16 June 2011) is also '**irresistible**' [irresistible]. *L'Oréal* Youth Code face cream (*Elle* UK August 2011) is 'so **luxurious**', whilst *Maybelline* Color Sensational lipgloss (*Cosmopolitan* UK August 2011) is described as available in '6 **luscious** shades'. In an advertisement for *Maybelline* Color Sensational lipstick (*Cosmopolitan* UK June 2011), the consumer is asked to 'see the **sumptuous** side of high shine'. *L'Oréal* Color Riche lipstick boasts '**couleurs éclatantes, voluptueuses**' [**dazzling, voluptuous** colours]. These kinds of examples focus on what we might term various Product Qualities, such as the texture, shine, or colour of the cosmetic. A pleasurable usage experience is emphasised. In a slightly different vein, the next section of analysis will consider the sensual *actions* of the cosmetic advertised.

Sensual Verbs: Product Actions

Cosmetics advertising copy often employs verbs that have connotations of a sensual nature to describe the action of the beauty product. A general formula that can be found is:

PRODUCT + VERB OF SENSUAL NATURE + BODY PART OF CONSUMER

In their discussions of subjective, affective language in female-targeted texts, Benwell and Stokoe (2006: 183) suggest that, in transitivity terms, the process is often Material and the product tends to be the Actor. The focus for analysis in this section will consider the sensual verb at the core of the Material process. Some examples from the data of these kinds of **Product Actions** and their formulas are outlined below (Table 4.1).

Table 4.1 Product Actions

Product and source	Sensual verb construction	Formula
Lancôme L'Absolu Nu lipstick (*Elle* UK May 2011)	**Embraces** your lips	Product + sensual verb + body part [Lipstick] + [embrace] + [lips]
Estée Lauder Pure Color Sensuous Rouge lipstick (*Elle* UK September 2011)	**Caresses** your lips	Product + sensual verb + body part [Lipstick] + [caress] + [lips]
Six Crème Redensifiante Nuit [Redensifying Night Cream] (*Elle* France 3 June 2011)	**drape** votre peau d'actfis apaisants et réparateurs [**drapes** your skin in soothing and repairing active ingredients]	Product + sensual verb + body part [Cream] + [drape] + [skin]
Estée Lauder Pure Color lipstick (original) (*Elle* UK May 2011)	It **leaves** your lips **wanting more**	Product + sensual verb + body part [Lipstick colour] + [leave wanting more] + [lips]
Nivea Lait Crème Nourrisant [Nourishing Body Milk] (*Elle* France 5 August 2011)	pour la **rendre douce comme une caresse** [**leaves** your skin as **soft as a caress**]	Product + sensual verb + body part [Body milk] + [leave soft as a caress] + [skin]
VO5 Argan Oil shampoo (*Cosmopolitan* UK September 2011)	[...] **leaves** hair **sensationally soft and shiny**	Product + sensual verb + body part [shampoo] + [leave sensationally soft and shiny] + [hair]

The variations of PRODUCT + VERB OF SENSUAL NATURE + BODY PART OF CONSUMER in the below examples reinforce the sensual action of the beauty product on the consumer's body. As with the category of Product Qualities, the connotation of these grammatical constructions is meant to be positive: using this beauty product will give your body a sensual or pleasurable experience. The evaluative language in these verb constructions reinforces the pleasurable action of the products advertised.

Sensual Discourse: Product Effects

Sensual or sensuous verbs and adjectives are often employed to describe the product's effect on the applicable body part, the body as a whole, and/or the female consumer as a unified entity. The sensual description may convey an appealing or desiring effect, which the consumer can then obtain through product purchase and usage (Table 4.2).

It should be noted that the consumer may already wish to achieve the effect of the product, for example, **sensuous** lips or **lush** eyelashes, but it is perhaps more likely that this may be a need or desire created, at least in

Table 4.2   Product Effects

Product and source	Product Effect(s)
Estée Lauder Pure Color Sensuous Rouge lipstick (*Elle* UK September 2011)	Lips have never felt this **sensuous**
Clarins Daily Energizers skin care (*Elle* UK September 2011)	Turmeric, alchemilla, gingko biloba – count on them all for clear, **lush**, luminous skin
Maybelline Color Sensational The Shine lipstick (*Elle* UK June 2011)	For lips that **flaunt** our most spectacular shine
Frank Provost soin sans-rinçage [leave-in hair care] (*Cosmopolitan* France July)	cheveux nourris jusqu'aux pointes, **sublimes**, faciles à coiffer [hair which is nourished right to the tips, **sublime**, and easy to style]
Maybelline Color Sensational Lipstain (*Elle* UK September 2011)	**Kiss** of colour for **lush** lips
Clarins HydraQuench Tinted Moisturiser (*Cosmopolitan* UK July 2011)	Skin feels **lusciously** fresh
L'Oréal Volume Million Lashes mascara (*Elle* UK September 2011)	Millionised lashes, beyond **lush**
Vichy Liftactiv skin care (*Elle* UK June 2011)	Skin feels **velvety smooth**
Nivea lait fluide [body lotion] (*Elle* France 27 May 2011)	une peau **irrésistible** [**irresistible** skin]

part, by the advertising copy. In a general sense, these descriptions of product effects link the cosmetic advertised to sensuality, but they may also make the product more appealing through the language used. The notion of femininity as a sensual identity is key here, as the various body parts of the women are described in sensual ways. All the consumer must do to achieve these desired effects is, seemingly, to buy and use the particular product. These descriptions of Product Effects could fit into Martin and White's (2005) Appraisal framework category of *appreciation*, in which lexical items represent the value of things.[5] For Product Effects, the advertisements tend to fit into the category of Reaction, as they emphasise aspects that may catch our attention or please us (Martin and White 2005: 56), such as **lush, velvety smooth**, and **irresistible** [**irresistible**] in the examples above. The category of Product Qualities also encompasses adjectives and adverbs of Reaction, such as **voluptueuses** [**voluptuous**] and **sumptuous**. The next section will consider sensual visual elements from the data, with a particular focus on how females in the advertisements are depicted in an overtly sensual manner.

Sensualised Imagery: Parted Lips

Parted lips, one of the visual sexual elements of 'beauty pornography' (Wolf 1991), will be analysed first. Popular books on body language suggest that a parted mouth or slightly open lips may be non-verbal indications of sexual arousal or orgasm (Lloyd-Elliot 2005: 92, 95; Givens 2006: 112). The implications of the use of parted lips in beauty advertising could be that the cosmetic will provide some kind of sexual pleasure to the consumer, or, perhaps more likely, this technique associates the product with sensuality in order to make it more attractive, which in turn may encourage purchase. In relation to the concept of *congruence* (the connection or lack thereof between the product and the manner in which it is advertised), lips would certainly be expected to feature in an advertisement for lipsticks, but they do not necessarily have to be parted in a sexualised manner. In addition, the use of a slightly open mouth occurs in advertising for many other products in which there is little or no congruence, such as shampoo or nail varnish. The use of slightly parted lips occurred in a range of product advertisements analysed, including *Dior* Be Iconic lipstick (*Cosmopolitan* France May 2011); *Estée Lauder* Pure Color Sensuous Rouge lipstick (*Cosmopolitan* UK September 2011); *Batiste* dry shampoo (*Cosmopolitan* UK September 2011); *Maybelline* Tenue et Strong Pro nail polish (*Elle* France 12 August 2011); *Max Factor* False Lash Effect Fusion mascara (*Elle* UK May 2011); *Max Factor* Smoky Eye Effect Eyeshadow

(*Cosmopolitan* UK May 2011); Aussie Lusciously Light 3 Minute Miracle deep conditioner (*Elle* UK July 2011); *Clairol* Perfect 10 hair colour (*Elle* UK July 2011); and *Estée Lauder* Idéalist sérum [serum] (*Elle* France 30 September). In many of these examples, parted lips are often accompanied by closed or lowered eyes. In the popular field of body language, these so-called 'bedroom eyes' are often used to signify sexual desire or arousal (Givens 2006: 102). Thus, these visual elements combine to heighten the potential sensual meaning of the advertisements in this category.

PRODUCT REPRESENTATIONS: SENSORY MODALITY

From the perspective of multimodality, low modality images tend to have less visual detail and be more abstract or connotative, whereas high modality images are linked more to real-life people, places, and situations (Kress and van Leeuwen 2006). Images with high naturalistic modality show images more or less as they would appear in real life. As such, modality values correspond with 'visual truths' in particular contexts (van Leeuwen 2005: 168). Generally, the closer an image is to its real-life counterpart, the higher the naturalistic modality (van Leeuwen 2005: 168). The concept of *sensory modality*, however, works in a slightly different way to naturalistic modality: with sensory modality, the 'visual truth' comes from the pleasure or displeasure created by imagery and manifested through an increased degree of naturalism. Colour, depth, light, shade, and so on may become exaggerated and 'more than real' (van Leeuwen 2005: 168). Sensory modality therefore makes objects or people appear 'better' than their real-life counterparts, as any flaws or irregularities in tone, texture, or colour are perfected.

Sensory modality is particularly significant for analysis of sensual or sexual images as it is often employed in domains where there is a focus on pleasure: for example, in beauty advertisements.[6] In contemporary cosmetics advertisements, there are many elements of sensory modality at play: colours appear richer; hair appears glossier; skin appears flawless. In addition to emphasising pleasure, sensory modality may also convey a sense of opulence and/or indulgence, often the case in the advertisements explored in this book. For example, in an advertisement for *Pantene* Pro-V Smooth & Sleek shampoo (*Elle* UK September 2011), the model's hair is in the centre of the advertisement and takes up a lot of space, immediately creating salience. The hair appears incredibly smooth and glossy, with a rich colour and a very high shine. The waves of the hair also appear to be exaggerated so that the image is reminiscent of a waterfall or cascade, which in turn highlights the sensory effect. The feeling of sensation is evoked through the use of modality, and there is of course also the basic presupposition that use of the brand of shampoo can make your hair look the good. Similarly, *Garnier* Ultra Doux shampooing à l'huile d'argan et cranberry [argan oil and cranberry shampoo] (*Elle* France 30 September 2011) does not include images of hair, but rather displayed visuals of the product ingredients in which the sensory modality is high. The cranberries certainly appear 'more than real' (van Leeuwen 2005: 168), with a very bright hue of red and a shiny, glossy effect. They are dripping with what we presume to be argan oil, the other advertised ingredient in the shampoo. The golden hue of the glistening oil evokes a sensation that characterises the product as explicitly opulent. Another example displaying high sensory modality is *Chanel* Sublimage La crème [face cream] (*Elle* France 10 June 2011). In typical *Chanel* style, the pictured packaging is minimalist yet decadent: a shiny glass jar with its black, glossy lid emblazoned with the *Chanel* logo. The centre of the jar is transparent, displaying its contents: a shimmering gold cream, with a high-reflective finish. In addition, the colours of the main image are reinforced by the white, gold, and black fonts used elsewhere in the advertisement, which are also the brand colours of *Chanel*.

NUDITY ACROSS CULTURES

Another visual manifestation of sensuality in contemporary cosmetics advertising is nudity. It may be considered somewhat stereotypical or cliChéd that the French are more comfortable with nudity, sexual images, and sexual references than, for example, Britain, Ireland, or North America. However, this phenomenon *is* generally borne out in the relevant literature. For example, Manceau and Tissier-Desbordes (2006) state there is often more nudity in French advertisements than in those of many other European countries. Biswas et al.'s (1992) research compared print advertising from the USA and France and found that the French advertisements included more sexual appeals, predominantly in the form of visuals. Issues surrounding use of the naked body in advertising material and, more broadly, in media contexts, are heavily intertwined with a particular society's view on the naked body, which has varied greatly over time and in relation to differing socio-religious contexts.[7]

With regard to the regulation of advertising content, the regulatory bodies introduced earlier in the book, the ASA (UK) and the ARPP

(France), and their related bodies, the CAP (Committee of Advertising Practice) and CEP (Conseil de l'Ethique Publicitaire: an ethics advisory board), provide specific advice on sexual imagery in advertising. The CEP acknowledges that France is generally more tolerant of public/media nudity than many of its European neighbours and explains that nudity is generally permitted, although various factors should be taken into account. In particular, advertising should not reduce human beings, especially women, to objects.[8] The UK's CAP advice cautions that while gratuitous[9] use of nudity can cause serious or widespread offence, tolerance is increased if there is a degree of congruence, that is, if the nudity is relevant to the product advertised. They give examples of lingerie and beauty advertisements in this context.[10] As suggested earlier, in some cases there may be a clear argument for congruence. For example, an advertisement for a body lotion could depict a woman in underwear applying the product. However, a model in underwear featuring in a nail varnish advertisement is not necessarily relevant to the product advertised. Even when there *is* feasibly some degree of congruence, the advertisement could still in theory be gratuitous, oversexualised, or provocative. In theory, highly sexualised ads in the UK can be withdrawn if there are a substantial number of complaints. The *medium* of advertising is also significant. The ASA, for example, has stricter guidelines on what sorts of images can be displayed on billboard hoardings, especially if near a school or a place of worship.[11] Arguably, print advertisements in a magazine publication targeted at adult females are perhaps less likely to be seen by very young children. The ASA has compiled a list of characteristics[12] that might be considered sexually suggestive and therefore deemed unsuitable for outdoor advertising (Table 4.3).

For the purposes of exploring nudity in the data compiled for this book, there are of course issues of classification. A rather wide-ranging definition has been applied, using the following criteria (numbers 4–6 have been taken from the ASA criteria given in Table 4.3) (Table 4.4).

Out of 246 English advertisements analysed for this book, 18 contained at least one element of nudity (using this broad criteria), which amounts to 7 %. On the other hand, 44 out of 249, or 18 %, of the French advertisements meet the criteria for nudity, demonstrating a higher degree of frequency. As with Chapter 3, a chi-square test was conducted to measure the significance of these different frequencies. The test resulted in a p value of 0.001, which means that the difference between the two groups is statistically significant at the 5 % margin of error. This increased use of nudity

Table 4.3   ASA list of characteristics unsuitable for outdoor advertising

1.	Poses suggestive of a sexual position: the parting of the legs, the accentuation of the hip etc.
2.	Amorous or sexually passionate facial expressions
3.	Exposure of breasts, including partial
4.	Poses such as hands on the hips, gripping of hair in conjunction with a sexually suggestive facial expression
5.	Images of touching oneself in a sexual manner, such as stroking the legs or holding/gripping the breasts
6.	Suggestion in facial or bodily expression of an orgasm
7.	Images of suggestive undressing, such as pulling down a bra strap or knickers
8.	Ads which draw undue attention to body parts, such as breasts or buttocks, in a sexual way
9.	Ads which show people in poses emulating a sexual position or alluding to sexual activity
10.	Overtly sexual lingerie such as stockings, suspenders or paraphernalia such as whips or chains

Table 4.4   Broad definition of nudity

1.	Conventional nudity, often with strategically placed items in the advertisement
2.	Implied nudity: for example, the shot of someone's nude back
3.	Very little clothing, such as underwear or a bikini
4.	Partial or full exposure of breasts
5.	Images of suggestive undressing
6.	Ads that draw attention to body parts in a sexually suggestive manner

in the French data supports Biswas et al.'s (1992) study mentioned earlier in the chapter, namely that there tend to be more visual sexual appeals in French than in UK advertising. The increased incidences of nudity in the French data are possibly related to a more relaxed attitude to nudity in French media culture, which is acknowledged and accepted by the ARPP. A further complicating factor in the use of the nudity is that sometimes it is arguably not used in a primarily sensual manner, but to show the effects of particular products in a visually 'scientific' format (for example, close-up shots of body parts). This phenomenon can be seen in particular in French advertisements for 'slimming creams', which often use a 'scientific' register and imagery to show measurable visual effects of the product to the consumer. These products are more popular in France, and their connection to 'scientific' discourse will be explored more fully in the following chapter. With this in mind, we can return to the questions posed at the beginning of this chapter surrounding whether nudity is always sexual in contemporary cosmetics advertisements. Another issue in this context, of course, concerns the use of airbrushing in the bodies represented in advertisements. Recently, some UK advertisements have been asked to withdraw or modify their imagery due to airbrushing of the models as it was considering misleading.[13] If the advertising company has used airbrushing to a large extent, the standard of femininity to which women could aspire may be far from realistic.

Sensual Discourse in French and English Advertisements

Having considered the frequency of *nudity* in the French and English data, the overall use of sensual language and imagery will now be addressed. For the English data, 169 out of 246 advertisements, or 69 %, contained sensual language and imagery. For the French data, 158 out of 249 advertisements, or 63 %, displayed this feature. Raw frequencies are therefore very similar in both languages. The chi-square test produced a p value of 0.218, which is above the 0.05 margin of error; consequently, the null hypothesis is not rejected and it is concluded that the difference has occurred by chance. Therefore, although the difference in nudity is statistically significant, the overall occurrence of sensual discourse is not. The French advertisements contain more nudity, but the English advertisements have slightly more sensual language and imagery overall. This might point towards similar patterns in the occurrence of sensual discourse in French and English cosmetics advertising, and may be a starting point for further research.

Sexual Innuendo: The Case of *Batiste*

The examples above have explored the discourse of sensation and sensuality commonly found in contemporary cosmetics advertisements. More explicit or blatant sexualised language or imagery, however, tends to be less frequent. One advertisement worthy of discussion because of the overt sexual innuendo is that of *Batiste* dry shampoo (*Cosmopolitan* UK September 2011). The advertisement features a female in her bedroom looking directly at the viewer (a 'demand' image, according to Kress and van Leeuwen's (2006) categories), with a smaller sub-set of images showing the model applying the dry shampoo advertised. The text on the left-hand page tells us, in a handwritten font, **I'm at it three times a week** while the right-hand side urges the reader: **Cheat on your everyday shampoo. A quick spray is all it takes to refresh your hair between washes, leaving it full of body and texture. What more could a busy woman want? Reveal all at batistehair.co.uk. Available at Boots, Superdrug, chemists and supermarkets.** Additionally, the advertisement contains a quotation from what is presumed to be a *Batiste* product user (although it is clear from the image that this is a model and not a 'real' consumer of the product). The female model in the advertisement tells the reader **I'm at it three times a week** which, in a British English context, has overtly sexual connotations as 'to be at it' can be a colloquial term for sexual activity. The other elements in the image reinforce the sexual innuendo: there is a door half-ajar with a partially hidden bed. This image may suggest that behind the door there is a female having sex, and the angle of the door in the shot makes it look like someone is coming through the door to discover a scene of sexual activity. This corresponds with the text **Cheat on your everyday shampoo**: 'sexual activity' can be refined further here to denote 'cheating on one's partner [by engaging in sex with someone else]'. The woman's mouth is slightly open, which, as discussed extensively earlier in the chapter, often suggests sexual arousal. The body language of the model may suggest a slight coyness or even a guilty pleasure: she is looking at the reader slightly over her shoulder and playing with her hair, which could be viewed as a sensual or provocative signal to the viewer (Lloyd-Elliot 2005: 103, 122, 136). Furthermore, other visual signs in the advertisement may have the meaning potential of recent sexual activity: there is a pale pink lace slip lying over a chair in the right-hand side of page 2, and the bed sheets on which the model is sitting are crumpled.

If we return to **Cheat on your everyday shampoo**, which further plays on the previous sexual innuendo and also may suggest promiscuity, the implied reading is that *Batiste* is a useful alternative to 'ordinary' shampoos. To take the analysis further, **Cheat on your everyday shampoo** can be analysed using Conceptual Metaphor Theory (CMT),[14] in which we have the conceptual metaphor formula SHAMPOO IS A SEXUAL PARTNER. The sexual innuendo is further reinforced by the sexualised images in the left-hand corner of the advertisement, which depict the model using the product in three small step-by-step pictures. In the second image her expression is sexually suggestive, with closed eyes and an open mouth as she applies the shampoo. In the third image, she appears contented after having used the product, and if we take the innuendo further, there could be an implication of sexual satisfaction. These images may recall the long-running *Herbal Essences* shampoo television and print advertisements (UK and US), which depict a female in the shower (or, in more recent iterations, an airplane bathroom) using the shampoo while shouting 'yes, yes, yes' in a simulation of orgasmic pleasure. The tagline used in the print advertisements was 'a totally organic experience', and the similarity of the word 'organic' to 'orgasmic' was surely a fact not overlooked by the advertisement copywriters. Like the *Batiste* advertisements, the high sexual innuendo may suggest a (sexual) pleasure that can be obtained from product usage. Arguably here, in addition to the linguistic analysis, the issue of congruence comes into question, as the reality of achieving an actual sexual pleasure from spraying a dry shampoo in one's hair is perhaps unlikely. Of course, the suggestion of this by the advertiser is likely to be somewhat tongue-in-cheek and/or humorous.

SEX APPEAL AND THE TARGET CONSUMER

Economic concerns over advertising sponsorship are no doubt a factor in the way in which magazines can express concerns over what they often class as the sexual objectification of women (such as prostitution, strip clubs, and Page 3 models) amidst a sea of cosmetics advertisements featuring semi-nude females with highly sexualised facial expressions. The economic impetus may also go some way to explain the rather strange phenomenon that is the appearance of advertisements containing sexualised, half-naked women in magazines with a predominantly heterosexual female demographic. In Gauntlett's (2008) Reader Response to magazines research, one of his participants, a 36-year-old female from London, commented upon the 'perversity' of women constantly looking at images of sexual, naked females, stating that she '[…] enjoy[ed] the polymorphous perversity of lots of images of gorgeous, naked or half-dressed or fantastically clad young women who present themselves for a gaze that is somewhere between objectification and identification but clearly can't be reduced to either' (Gauntlett 2008: 208). Beyond these notions of objectification and identification, perhaps the images of naked women could also be viewed as in some way aspirational or inspirational for the female viewer: she may aim to attain their standards of beauty, and the promise of sexuality and/or sensuality that goes with it. Of course, the media and its influence on body image is a hugely complex debate, but it can be generally agreed that these images may have some impact on a large number of women. Even for women who claim to be unaffected, it is still significant that these are the images on display within the media in their society, culture, and, quite often, on their bedside table.[15]

If we consider Reader Response in a little more detail, Dudley's (1999) research into consumer attitudes towards nudity in US advertising found that increased nudity was often seen as offensive but was also a useful technique for attracting the consumer's attention. Use of nudity often helped brands to differentiate themselves from others (Dudley 1999: 94). Interestingly, however, nude models were viewed by the study participants as more favourable than the topless models. Although the study does not provide conclusive suggestions on why this is the case, it could perhaps be due to some negative connotations associated with topless glamour models. In Beetles and Harris' (2005) study of UK consumer attitudes towards female nudity in advertising, the issue of congruence was a key factor in determining positive or negative reactions from the reader response group. Participants were often irritated or angered by the apparent lack of congruence for some of the products (Beetles and Harris 2005: 416–419). In addition, the notion that 'sex sells' may not necessarily be the case, as participants in Beetles and Harris' study appeared to be bored by advertisers' frequent use of female nudity, leading the authors of the study to conclude that female nudity in advertising may be overused and therefore may not attain the desired positive consumer reaction. Manceau and Tissier-Desbordes (2006) found that French female consumers and older people were generally less tolerant of higher levels of sex and nudity in advertising. Nudity, therefore, in its various forms, may produce mixed results for the target consumer. However, as the abundance of examples throughout this chapter has demonstrated, sensualised discourse more generally appears to be a salient feature of contemporary English and French cosmetics advertising discourse.

As suggested in this chapter, contemporary beauty advertisements feature sexually attractive women in addition to describing their products in a sensual manner, especially with regard to the pleasurable sensations that can apparently be derived from product usage. Although nudity did appear more frequently in the French data and this difference was statistically significant, on the whole, sensual discourse had similar frequencies of occurrence in both the English and French advertisements analysed. This may suggest that sensual discourse is employed in both French and English cosmetics advertising contexts, but that the English sensual discourse may contain other elements in lieu of the nudity in a French context. The potential Reader Response to sensuality in cosmetics advertising discourse is complex. The consumer may find the sensuality of beauty advertisements appealing, unrealistic, or offensive (or, at times, even a combination of all three). However, it is clear that the models of femininity on offer in contemporary cosmetics advertising discourse emphasise sensuality: both of females themselves and of the beauty products advertised.

NOTES

1. More information available at https://nomorepage3.wordpress.com/
2. Of course, a desire to look sexually appealing to others can be understood and even seen as a 'natural' part of the human experience (although possible biological links to reproduction in this context are not entirely straightforward). The issue, however, is the somewhat restrictive representation of female sensuality often found in the media, which positions some females as outside of the advertising norm. These sexualised images are often contextually detached and linked to narcissism, with models caressing their own skin, admiring themselves in the mirror, and so on (Kilbourne 2003: 174–175).
3. A related issue is that the images of sexuality displayed in advertising and other media domains may be far removed from the reality of 'ordinary' people's sex lives. Penny (2011: 9) mentions the *Beautiful Agony* website in which a range of people can upload and share photos and videos of their face at the point of orgasm, with the subsequent diversity of expressions strongly suggesting that the media presentation of a closed-eye, open-mouthed (hetero)sexual female apparently experiencing intense sexual pleasure may bear little or no relation to the average person's sexual encounters. Furthermore, the media link between a predominantly white, attractive, able-bodied, thin, heterosexual woman and sexual experience may be alienating to many women who do not fit easily into these categories (see for example Gill 2009: 104). Similarly, even if there exist females who *do* correspond to the sexual feminine media ideal, this does not necessarily make these women feel more 'sexy' or entail that they are having more or better sex than those excluded from media representations.
4. This so-called Midriff Advertising has four major themes: 'an emphasis on the body, a shift from objectification to sexual subjectification, a pronounced discourse of choice and autonomy, and an emphasis on empowerment' (Gill 2009: 99).
5. As noted in Chapter 3, Bednarek (2009) has suggested that this framework could benefit from more refining.

6. See van Leeuwen (2005: 170) for additional examples of sensory modality.
7. For a good historical overview of the naked body, see Carr-Gomm (2012).
8. Their advice from this can be found at http://www.cep-pub.org/Avis-sur-la-nudite-en-publicite.html
9. What constitutes gratuitous may certainly be a matter of debate.
10. More information on this at https://www.cap.org.uk/Advice-Training-on-the-rules/Advice-Online-Database/Offence-Nudity.aspx#.Vu67veKdC70
11. Full statement available at https://www.asa.org.uk/News-resources/Media-Centre/2011/ASA-statement-on-sexual-imagery-in-outdoor-advertising.aspx#.Vu7Ja-KdC70
12. Advice from https://www.cap.org.uk/Advice-Training-on-the-rules/Advice-Online-Database/~/media/Files/ASA/Misc/Outdoor%20Advertising%20Statement%20for%20Industry.ashx
13. The ASA website (https://www.asa.org.uk) tends to put up recent examples of these on a regular basis.
14. See Lakoff and Johnson (2003) for more on CMT; see Forceville (1996, 2013) for examples of this in advertising.
15. See Orbach (2010) for more on media culture and body image.

REFERENCES

Attwood, F. (2009). *Mainstreaming sex: The sexualisation of Western culture.* New York: IB Tauris.

Banyard, K. (2011). *The equality illusion: The truth about men and women today.* London: Faber and Faber.

Beauvoir, S. de. (1997). The second sex (Translated from the French by Parshley, H. Original French version 1949). London: Vintage.

Bednarek, M. (2009). Language patterns and attitude. *Functions of Language, 16*(2), 165–192.

Beetles, A., & Harris, L. (2005). Consumer attitudes to female nudity in advertising: An empirical study. *Marketing Theory, 5*(4), 397–432.

Benwell, B., & Stokoe, E. (2006). *Discourse and identity.* Edinburgh: Edinburgh University Press.

Biswas, A., Olsen, J., & Carlet, V. (1992). A comparison of print advertisements from the United States and France. *Journal of Advertising, 21*(4), 73–81.

Buckingham, D. (2011). *The material child: Growing up in consumer culture.* Cambridge: Polity Press.

Buckingham, D., & Bragg, S. (2004). *Young people, sex and the media: The facts of life?* Basingstoke: Palgrave Macmillan.

Carr-Gomm, P. (2012). *A brief history of nakedness.* London: Reaktion Books.

Dudley, S. (1999). Consumer attitudes toward nudity in advertising. *Journal of Marketing Theory and Practice, 7*(4), 89–96.

Durham, M. G. (2009). *The Lolita effect: The media sexualisation of young girls and what we can do about it.* London: Gerard Duckworth and Company.

Forceville, C. (1996). *Pictorial metaphor in advertising.* London: Routledge.

Forceville, C. (2013). The strategic use of the visual mode in advertising metaphors. In E. Djonov & S. Zhao (Eds.), *Critical multimodal studies of popular culture* (pp. 55–70). New York: Routledge.

Gauntlett, D. (2008). *Media, gender and identity: An introduction* (2nd ed.). London: Routledge.

Gill, R. (2007). *Gender and the media.* Cambridge: Cambridge University Press.

Gill, R. (2009). Supersexualize me! Advertising, (post) feminism and "the mid-riffs". In F. Attwood (Ed.), *Mainstreaming sex: The sexualisation of Western culture.* New York: IB Tauris.

Givens, D. (2006). *Love signals: A practical field guide to the body language of courtship.* New York: St. Martin's Press.

Goldman, R. (1992). *Reading ads socially.* London/New York: Routledge.

Greer, G. (1971). *The female eunuch.* London: Paladin.

Jeffries, L. (2007). *The textual construction of the female body: A critical discourse analysis approach.* Basingstoke: Palgrave Macmillan.

Kilbourne, J. (2003). Advertising and disconnection. In T. Reichert & J. Lambiase (Eds.), *Sex in advertising: Perspectives on the erotic appeal* (pp. 173–180). Mahwah: Lawrence Erlbaum.

Kress, G., & van Leeuwen, T. (2006). *Reading images: The grammar of visual design* (2nd ed.). London: Routledge.

Lakoff, G., & Johnson, M. (2003). *Metaphors we live by.* Chicago: University of Chicago Press.

Lazar, M. (2006). "Discover the power of femininity!" Analysing global "power femininity" in local advertising. *Feminist Media Studies: New Femininities, 6*(4), 505–517.

Levy, A. (2006). *Female chauvinist pigs: Women and the rise of raunch culture.* London: Pocket.

Lloyd-Elliot, M. (2005). *The secrets of sexual body language.* London: Hamlyn.

Machin, D., & Thornborrow, J. (2003). Branding and discourse: The case of Cosmopolitan. *Discourse and Society, 1*(4), 453–471.

Manceau, D., & Tissier-Desbordes, E. (2006). Are sex and death taboos in advertising? An analysis of taboos in advertising and a survey of French consumer perceptions. *International Journal of Advertising, 25*(1), 9–33.

Martin, J., & White, P. (2005). *The language of evaluation: Appraisal in English.* Basingstoke: Palgrave Macmillan.

McNair, B. (2002). *Striptease culture: Sex, media and the democratization of desire.* London: Routledge.

Mills, S. (1995). *Feminist stylistics.* London: Routledge.

Orbach, S. (2010). *Bodies.* London: Profile.

Orenstein, P. (2011). *Cinderella ate my daughter.* New York: Harper.

Penny, L. (2011). *Meat market: Female flesh under capitalism.* London: Zero Books.

van Leeuwen, T. (2005). *Introducing social semiotics.* London: Routledge.

Walter, N. (2010). *Living dolls: The return of sexism.* London: Virago.

Waters, M. (2007). Sexing it up? Women, pornography and third wave feminism. In S. Gillis, G. Howie, & R. Munford (Eds.), *Third wave feminism: A critical exploration* (2nd ed., pp. 250–265). Basingstoke: Palgrave Macmillan.

Wolf, N. (1991). *The beauty myth: How images of beauty are used against women.* London: Vintage.

CHAPTER 5

Scientised Beauty Advertising Discourse: *With Peptides* or *Paraben-Free?*

Abstract A common technique in contemporary beauty advertisements is the use of various 'scientific' claims, lexis, and imagery. This chapter identifies, and compares, some common 'scientised' discursive strategies in French and English beauty advertising, aiming to provide a more concrete framework for analysing this aspect of cosmetics advertising. The chapter finishes by addressing a more recent counter-phenomenon: a 'green' cosmetics advertising discourse, in which brands emphasise a lack of chemicals and a more 'natural' approach to beauty.

Keywords Advertising across cultures • Scientific language • Green beauty

BEAUTY MEETS SCIENCE

The previous chapters have explored the construction of 'problems' in beauty advertising (**dry skin, flat hair, wrinkled eyes**) and the emphasis placed on the positive sensory experience of using cosmetics (**creamy texture, caresses lips**). Another technique that can be found in beauty advertisements is the use of various 'scientific' claims, lexis, and imagery.

Some of the material in this chapter appeared previously in Ringrow (2014).

Perhaps in an attempt to differentiate their products in an ever-growing market, brands are turning to science to help authenticate beauty products. This is a phenomenon that can be seen through references to DNA, cell coding, systems, and formulas, in addition to ingredients such as hyaluronic acid and bioactive glycoproteins. This kind of discourse can be found not only in advertisements themselves but also in advertorials and magazine features, which may enable the producer of the text to sound authoritative on a certain topic (Jeffries 2007). The use of 'scientific' language is especially prevalent in anti-ageing skincare, where it aims to imbue the products with a sense of authenticity and perhaps a guarantee of effectiveness (Coupland 2003, 2007). Connections are made between cosmetics and overall health and well-being, suggesting that products are akin to medico-scientific tools (Harrison 2008, 2012).

Increased use of 'scientific' language in beauty advertisements may be indicative of the broader growing trend of so-called 'cosmeceuticals': a blend of 'cosmetic' and 'pharmaceutical', which is often used to describe a cosmetic with drug-like benefits.[1] In many countries, there is a legal distinction between drugs and cosmetics in that drugs are products that cure, treat, mitigate, or prevent disease or that affect the structure or function of the human body. Cosmetics, however, do not. An example of what could constitute a cosmeceutical is an alpha hydroxy acid (AHA): an exfoliant that can remove the surface layer of skin (a drug-like result) to treat scars, wrinkles, acne, and lighten skin.[2] It would therefore perhaps be expected for advertising for AHAs and other cosmeceutical products to contain some scientific language due to the nature of the cosmetic being advertised. However, this discourse increasingly occurs in the majority of contemporary cosmetics advertisements, most of which are not for cosmeceuticals. In some ways, the use of scientific-sounding language could be seen as a slightly unusual technique in beauty advertising as there is not always necessarily a clear level of congruence between the scientific register and the cosmetic being promoted. The presence of scientific or scientific-sounding lexis in advertisements is related to the Problem-Solution discourse in Chapter 3, as 'solutions' can be presented using scientific vocabulary. This will be discussed in more detail later in the chapter.

This chapter identifies some common 'scientific' discursive strategies employed in French and English beauty advertising. In doing so, it aims to provide a more concrete framework for analysing cosmetics advertising discourse. The chapter finishes by addressing a more recent counter-phenomenon: a 'green' cosmetics advertising discourse, in which brands emphasise a lack of chemicals and a more 'natural' approach to skincare. Finding an appropriate terminology to discuss these kinds of issues is, however, somewhat problematic. Deciding whether the claims in advertising are actually *scientific* (if we understand scientific here to mean based on rigorous scientific research and methods) or simply *scientific-sounding* (if we understand this to mean suggestive of science but potentially exaggerated and/or misleading) is often difficult to ascertain for a number of complex reasons. If an advertisement claims that a product contains a particular ingredient and that ingredient does indeed have many benefits when tested in a laboratory, here we could certainly have a case for scientific (and not simply scientific-sounding) language. For many ingredients, however, their inclusion in a skin cream may have little to no effect. As higher concentrations of certain powerful ingredients may irritate and damage skin's outer layer, legal regulation may insist that only low levels be included in cosmetics formulas, potentially rendering the results less effective. Cosmetics companies are not currently required by law to display the dose or concentration on the label, although ingredients are in order of highest proportion first (Goldacre 2009: 22), and large doses of certain ingredients may not be practical for manufacturers as they could make the cost prohibitive. Additionally, the cream may not have been tested on human skin, and therefore topical applications could, in theory, offer little benefit. In this context, the promotion of a particular ingredient may be said to fall into the category of a more scientific-sounding discourse. Beauty companies are not necessarily being dishonest in terms of what their product contains, but results cannot always be guaranteed for a particular product based on inclusion of one ingredient (Goldacre 2009: 23). Claims on advertising copy apply to the entire product, not just the key or active ingredients mentioned. If a facial moisturiser has a claim such as 'contains collagen—skin hydration is improved after only one application', this could imply that *collagen* is the main factor in its hydrating benefits, which may not necessarily be the case, as other ingredients (often much cheaper and making up a larger percentage of the product) could contribute to the moisturising qualities (Goldacre 2009: 25).

The advertising copy may lead the consumer to believe that our body, skin, and hair require various ingredients for proper cell turnover, growth, function, and vitality, but this is not necessarily the case. Goldacre (2009: 24) argues that advertising references to creams containing DNA to improve cell renewal and/or turnover are dubious: DNA is a huge molecule that skin may not even be able to absorb, and moisturising creams cannot actually affect cell production or metabolism—although advertisements' suggestions that a product 'may help' stimulate cells are probably vague enough to potentially be true (Romanowski 2011: 65). As mentioned in Chapter 1, the terms used in advertising tend to be largely compliant with the guidelines set out by the advertising regulatory bodies, the ASA (UK) and the ARPP (France), but this does not mean that the language used is unproblematic in terms of what the consumer may infer about the product based on the emphasis on a particular ingredient or formula in the advertisement.

With regard to the actual scientific research behind the product advertising claims, this can also be difficult to determine. In some cases, the only studies that exist are those commissioned by the brand itself or the industry, which inevitably raise potential issues of bias. In addition, this research is not always retrievable in published academic forms. There is, undoubtedly, a huge range of research into beauty products, but the real lack of availability, transparency, and independent studies means it is often difficult to evaluate claims made on the advertising copy (Goldacre 2009: 21–23). Potential consumers may lack the time and/or inclination to fully investigate these issues for themselves: it is not entirely feasible to expect people outside of academia, or even outside of science departments, to spend their free time engaging with peer-reviewed cosmetics science journals. There is, however, a growing wealth of popular resources (from experts and interested laypeople alike) devoted to exploring the claims made in cosmetics advertisements, suggesting an increasing desire for useful information on this topic so that consumers can make informed decisions.[3]

When examining a cosmetics advertisement, it can therefore be difficult (both at first glance and even after much investigation) to determine whether it is scientific or simply scientific-sounding. In some cases, we might even go so far as to say the language seems to be 'pseudo-scientific'. However, the adjective 'pseudo-scientific' could have overtly negative connotations in terms of much-debated domains such as homeopathy, phrenology, and reflexology, and it may not necessarily be appropriate to equate cosmetics advertising with these fields. We can see these connotations in the following Key Word in Context (KWIC) concordance from the Corpus of Contemporary American English (COCA) (Davies, 2008–) , which includes the following examples: '[....] the archaic system of pseudo-scientific racial labelling'; '[...] racist, pseudo-scientific Hutu antiTutuism'; and '[...] truly homophobic and pseudo-scientific books on AIDS' (Fig. 5.1).

Taking into consideration these issues of terminology, throughout this chapter I use the term 'scientised' (following Coupland 2003, 2007, after Chaiken 1987) to mean using a register associated with science, regardless of whether it is merited or not. This scientised discourse, as illustrated in the following examples, helps to reinforce the idea that skincare is a serious business, and 'highly technologized products' can have measurable effects on physical appearance (Coupland 2007: 56). The following sections aim to categorise in more detail this type of scientised discourse prevalent in cosmetics advertisements.

1	AmSpect	"reports about missile defence, they offer much the same	**pseudo-scientific**	arguments as they did against Star Wars.
2	WashMonth	But considering that plenty of truly homophobic and	**pseudo-scientific**	books on AIDS sell like hotcakes
3	PopScience	compressed to a higher density, a popular goal in certain	**pseudo-scientific**	circles. It should have made clear
4	Atlantic	with the best care and treatment possible. Hitchens's	**pseudo-scientific**	claims about the significance and validity
5	ChristCentury	like its counterparts quadroon and octoroon- connotes the	**pseudo-scientific**	classification of the slave era.
6	ArtAmerica	overly obscure investigations of cultural clichs. Using a	**pseudo-scientific**	format, he presents such "studies" as
7	ChristCentury	any more than Rwandan Christianity produced racist,	**pseudo-scientific**	Hutu antiTutuism. But a misunderstanding
8	USAToday	this assessment. Charles Darwin's discoveries are called "	**pseudo-scientific**	ideas" that "tore away the moral
9	NatlReview	was to discipline those utopianisms and give them a	**pseudo-scientific**	purchase upon the inevitable 'course of
10	NewRepublic	not only racial preferences but the archaic system of	**pseudo-scientific**	racial labeling – for the best liberal
11	PopMech	that claim to improve fuel economy for various	**pseudo-scientific**	reasons. None have helped, and some
12	Ebony	further reinforced and given credibility by a plethora of	**pseudo-scientific**	sociological studies which

Fig. 5.1 Concordance for 'pseudo-scientific' from COCA, magazines category

Scientised Ingredients

References to particular ingredients, presumed to be of benefit to the skin, hair, body, and so on, help to create the scientised feel of many contemporary beauty advertisements. Advertisements often emphasise one or two main ingredients used in their product formulations. For example:

[Formule anti-choc au] **pro-silicium** [**pro-silicum**] (*Bourjois* Vernis 10 Jours [10-Day Nail Polish], *Elle* France 22 June 2011)

Glycoprotéines bioactives [**Bioactive glycoproteins**] (*Six* Crème Nuit Régénérante [Regenerating Night Cream], *Elle* France 6 May 2011)

La viniférine [**viniferine**] (*Claudalie* Vinoperfect [anti-ageing moisturiser], *Elle* France 8 July 2011)

Peptide biotechnologique [**Biotechnological peptide**] (*Lierac* Body-Slim soin minceur [slimming cream], *Cosmopolitan* France May 2011)

Le Super Acide Hyaluronique-Bio [**Organic super hyaluronic acid**] (*Shiseido* WrinkleResist 24, *Elle* France 17 July 2011)

Arguably, the consumer does not necessarily know (certainly not without perhaps searching online) what these ingredients do or why they may be necessary and/or effective. Their function is often elaborated on in the body copy of the advertisement, which may outline the ingredient and its benefit. For example:

Improved efficacy with 5X more **Hyaluronic Acid, an ingredient** produced naturally in the skin **that binds with moisture to give a plumping effect** (*Eucerin* Hyaluron-Filler day cream, *Elle* UK September 2011)

At other times, the ingredients may refer to a combination of possible ingredients, which are implied to have positive results. This strategy could make the product appear even more beneficial in that it is not simply one ingredient on its own, but rather an effective combination:

Anti-pollution and anti-oxidant ingredients (*Neutrogena* Multi-Defence Daily Moisturiser, *Cosmopolitan* UK June 2011)

A cocktail of minerals and plant extracts (*Clarins* Skin Illusion Foundation, *Cosmopolitan* UK May 2011)

A unique blend of peeling active ingredients (*Vichy* Normaderm Tri-Activ Anti-Imperfection Hydrating Care, *Cosmopolitan* UK May 2011)

Some ingredients are patented and/or have been (re)named by the company, which adds to the scientised register, perhaps suggesting a sense of exclusivity. Short descriptions of what the ingredient actually is can sometimes be found in the advertising copy. For example, **LR2412** (*Lancôme* Visionnaire LR2412 4%, *Elle* France 9 September 2011) is explained as **une molécule** [a molecule] in the main body of the advertisement, whereas **Pro-Gen®** (*L'Oréal* Youth Code face cream and serum, *Cosmopolitan* May UK 2011) is not, but in the context of the advertisement the consumer infers that it is an ingredient linked in some way to DNA or skin regeneration. As discussed earlier in the chapter, these ingredients might not always be effective in a cream format, due to low concentrations or issues with storage. Nonetheless, their presence in a beauty advertisement is used as a persuasive strategy to help convince the consumer that their products do actually work effectively due to these active ingredients.

SCIENTISED PRODUCT NAMES

In addition to the scientific-sounding product ingredients, the names of products themselves often have connotations of science. This may be a deliberate approach by the brand to bestow upon their product associations of science and consequentially authenticity and connections to research. Examples include:

Lierac **Body-Slim Concentré Multi-Action** [Body-Slim Multi-Action Concentrate] (*Cosmopolitan* France May 2011)

Shiseido **WrinkleResist 24** (skincare range) (*Elle* France 17 July 2011)

Lancôme **Visionnaire LR2412 4%** [anti-ageing treatment] (*Elle* France 9 September 2011)

E45 **DermaRestore Endless Moisture** body lotion (*Elle* UK August 2011)

Garnier **ExfoBrusher** (*Cosmopolitan* UK July 2011)

Lancôme **Génifique Activateur de Jeunesse** [Youth Activating Concentrate Serum] (*Elle* France 20 May 2011)

L'Oréal **Lash Architect 4D** mascara (*Cosmopolitan* UK June 2011)

Palmer's **Cocoa Butter Formulas** (*Cosmopolitan* UK June 2011)

Clinique **Pore Refining Solutions** (*Cosmopolitan* UK September 2011)

L'Oréal **Revitalift Total Repair 10** (*Elle* France 16 August 2011)

These scientific-sounding product names are especially frequent in higher-end skincare brands that attempt to consistently emphasise their links to scientific research and general health in their brand literature as a whole. Three such brands are *Vichy*, *Eucerin*, and *Clinique*, and some examples of their product names are listed below:

Vichy **Normaderm Tri-Activ Anti-Imperfection Hydrating Care** (*Cosmopolitan* UK May 2011)

Clinique **Even Better Concentré Anti-Taches correction teint** [official translation: **clinical dark spot corrector**] (*Cosmopolitan* France May 2011)

Vichy **Liftactiv Derm Source skincare** (*Elle* UK June 2011)

Eucerin **Hyaluron-Filler Jour** [**Hyaluron-Filler Day cream**] (*Elle* France 13 May 2011)

Vichy **Liftactiv 10 sérum** [serum] (*Elle* France 18 September 2011)

Eucerin **AQUAporin Active moisturising cream** (*Elle* UK May 2011)

For these brands in particular, the connection between cosmetics and science is an integral component of their marketing strategies. *Eucerin*'s current slogan is 'skin science that shows' and the brand website contains a section outlining 'our philosophy of dermo-cosmetic skin care',[4] displaying lexis of 'a medico-scientific register or voice' (Fairclough 1992: 171–176). Similarly, *Vichy*'s website[5] has an 'Ideal Skin Diagnostic' where users can complete questions and receive a diagnosis and advice on relevant products. *Clinique* has several similar diagnostic tools on its website,[6] corresponding to other aspects of their branding such as minimalist packaging and the white lab coats of their employees. These diagnostic tools have much in common with the discourse of medical consultations, with the site performing the role of expert, providing suitable advice and recommending treatments to the patient-consumer.

MEASURES OF VERIFIABILITY

Figures and statistics are often associated with a scientific or technical register. These can be employed to emphasise the concentration of the product's active ingredient. For example:

10x more concentrated in Pro-Gen® (*L'Oréal* Youth Code face cream and serum, *Cosmopolitan* UK May 2011)

5x PLUS d'Acide Hyaluronique [5 times more Hyaluronic Acid] (*Eucerin* Hyaluron-Filler Jour [Hyaluron-Filler Day cream], *Elle* France 13 May 2011)

La caféine active dosée à 10%, combinée à l'extrait de sureau [10% strength caffeine combined with elderberry extract] (*Lierac* Body-Slim soin minceur [slimming cream], *Elle* France 20 May 2011)

Caféine pure 3% [3% pure caffeine] (*Vichy* Aqua-Destock [slimming cream], *Cosmopolitan* France May 2011)

This strategy of focusing on the concentrations may be a way for brands to emphasise the potential effectiveness of their product, although arguably these percentages are not necessarily easy to interpret: for example, is 3 % caffeine a large dose? Will it translate into benefits for skin? The consumer is presumably expected to respond positively to these figures, but there may be a potential lack of clarity.

Statistics are often employed to express how many women were satisfied with the product's results in brand trials or tests. For example:

> **94% des femmes recommanderaient ce produit à leurs amies [94% of women would recommend this product to their friends]** (*Lierac* Body-Slim soin minceur [slimming cream], *Elle* France 20 May 2011)

The consumer should however be somewhat cautious of these types of statistics, as the number of women in the test group can vary enormously according to the product advertised. There is now a legal requirement to mention the numbers in the groups tested. For example, an advertisement for *Aveeno* Skin Relief lotion states:

> **90% of women felt their skin was more soothed and hydrated after only one day** (*Aveeno* Skin Relief lotion, *Cosmopolitan* May UK 2011)

The asterisk at the bottom clarified that this was 90 % of 191 women, which translates to 172 women. For comparative purposes, another advertisement for *Lancôme* Visionnaire LR2412 4% anti-ageing serum claimed the product was

> **[...] si puissant que plus d'1 femme sur 2 tentée par une intervention esthétique a l'intention de la reporter [so powerful that more than half of women considering a cosmetic procedure said they would delay it]** (*Lancôme* Visionnaire LR2412 4% [anti-ageing treatment], *Elle* France 9 September 2011)

The advertisement stated that this referred to 34 women; therefore 17 women in total said they would delay having cosmetic surgery due to using this product. These kinds of statistics may have been deliberately chosen and worded to present the product in a particular light. The use of '1 in 2' is a natural frequency, which may be more easily understood and assimilated, as opposed to percentages (Goldacre 2009: 257). If the sample groups are small, this has the potential to make any good consumer experiences in trials appear disproportionate in the percentages. Of course, this does not discredit the positive consumer reviews, but perhaps the smaller numbers do not always translate well into statistics. From a marketing perspective, positive test results can be used to convince company employees and executives '[...] that the cream merits the money and effort that will be put behind it' (Tungate 2011: 143).

Other statistics in cosmetics advertisements focus on how long the product's effects last, how well the product can perform, or its originality. For example:

Anti-frizz 48 heures [48 hours Anti-frizz] (*Elsève* Liss-Intense shampoo and conditioner, *Cosmopolitan* France August 2011)

80% more colour radiance protection (according to brand testing) (*L'Oréal* Elvive Colour Protect, *Elle* UK June 2011)

préserve l'éclat pendant 7 semaines [preserves colour for 7 weeks] (according to brand testing) (*Dessange* Réveil'Color [Colour Revitalise shampoo], *Elle* France 13 May 2011)

20 brevets déposés [20 patents pending] (*Lancôme* Visionnaire LR2412 4% [anti-ageing treatment], *Elle* France 9 September 2011)

À 28 jours: Silhouette affinée [After 28 days: a toned figure] (*Vichy* Aqua-Destock [slimming cream], *Cosmopolitan* France May 2011)

1 seule application par jour suffit pour 24h d'efficacité [Once-a-day application remains effective for 24 hours] (*Elancyl* Offensive Cellulite [cellulite cream], *Elle* France 19 August 2011)

In this way, product information can be presented in a more 'mathematical' format. The use of a 'linguistic disclaimer' can sometimes be found in relation to these figures. For example:

Lasts **up to** 24 hours (*Maybelline* The Falsies mascara, *Cosmopolitan* UK July 2011).

In theory, therefore, this complex prepositional phrase would suggest that the product could last one hour and the sentence would be true at a basic propositional level. However, the implicature is likely to be that the product lasts a long time: if not 24 hours, then certainly close to this length. This is not to say that this particular product does *not* last for 24 hours; however, more generally this kind of linguistic ambiguity may enable advertisers to make increased claims about their products. The decision to mention an actual timeframe (*24 hours*), as opposed to simply stating an alternative such as 'long-lasting', may create what Coupland (2007: 56) terms 'empirical verifiability': an attempt at a more concrete form of measurement in beauty advertisements.

PRODUCT SPECIFICATIONS

Another element of scientised discourse in cosmetics advertisements is an emphasis on product features and product design. Advertisements often highlight that the product has been well-designed, thus improving its overall efficacy. With regard to the Problem-Solution discourse discussed in Chapter 3, often the text on product design and features emphasises a design flaw or problem which is then solved. In some cases, consumers may or may not be aware of the problem's existence before viewing the advertisement: the excess mascara wiper on the mascara brush tube (to avoid messy spillage and wastage of product); the pump bottle (for accurately measuring the amount of product necessary for one application); foundations with attached brushes (to improve the finish of the make-up and avoid orange hands); facial cleansers with bristles (to disperse product and exfoliate the skin). By extrapolation, other products that do not have these features may be viewed as more wasteful, less user-friendly, and inadequately designed. Elements of product design and features tend to take the form of nouns or nominal phrases, as the following examples demonstrate:

Pointe biseautée [Slanted tip: on applicator brush] (*Bourjous* Vernis 10 Jours [10-Day Nail Polish], *Elle* France 22 June 2011)

Ultra-wide micro-diffusion spray (*Garnier* Sublime Bronze self-tan, *Cosmopolitan* UK June 2011)

La 1ère brosse millioniser [The first Millioniser brush] (*L'Oréal* Volume Million Lashes mascara, *Elle* France 13 May)

Our 1st pen applicator (*Maybelline* Color Sensational Lipstain, *Cosmopolitan* UK September 2011)

Spoon brush (*Maybelline* The Falsies mascara, *Cosmopolitan* UK July 2011)

Application gets easy: non drip mousse. As easy to apply as a shampoo (*L'Oréal Casting Crème* Sublime Mousse hair colour, *Cosmopolitan* UK July 2011)

These examples emphasise innovative product packing and design, which create the impression of enabling the consumer to get the best out of that particular cosmetic. This can also be created using visuals. For example, in the advertisement for *Estée Lauder* Advanced Night Repair sérum [serum] (*Cosmopolitan* France May 2011), the product applicator is shaped like a pipette, similar to that found in a laboratory, therefore suggesting precision of the required dosage. In a similar vein, *Garnier* Ultra Lift moisturiser (*Elle* France 6 May 2011) advertises that skin's improvement can be tracked with a 'wrinkle reader': a small cardboard strip that depicts different stages of wrinkles decreasing after so many days of product application. When this product launched, consumers in France and the UK could claim free samples along with this 'wrinkle reader'. The photographs on this particular advertisement and the related 'wrinkle reader' are not the normal perfected images we might expect in the domain of beauty advertising. Rather, they display what Kress and van Leeuwen (2006: 158) identify as 'high naturalistic modality', in which there is an increased level of correspondence between reality and the image depiction. In this context, there are wrinkles and shading on the model's skin in the advertisements. The decreasing appearance of wrinkles in the different steps in the 'reader', however, are more suggestive of lower modality. This kind of visual detailing are increase the pathologisation of ageing (Coupland 2007: 46–47) as women are encouraged to try the product and compare their skin progress with the images on the reader.

SCIENTISED SOLUTIONS IN FRENCH AND ENGLISH

This kind of scientific discourse was prevalent in both the English and French advertisements analysed. The French data contained 166 out of 249 advertisements displaying scientised language (67 %) whilst the English data contained 118 out of 246 advertisements (48 %). As in Chapters 3 and 4, a chi-square test was applied to determine whether these differences were statistically significant. The result was a p value of 0.001, which is less than the 5 % significance level, suggesting that there is a statistically significant difference between the French and English advertisements analysed here. If we consider why the French advertisements tend to employ more of this kind of language, one possible explanation for this phenomenon is the predominance of 'slimming creams' ('crèmes/produits minceur') and other related topical body firming and toning treatments in France. These are on the rise in the UK, but the French market is much larger, which is also reflected by the number and type of these creams on offer in France. One 2004 newspaper article estimated that whilst British women spend up to £30 million a year on slimming creams, the French market was worth £50 million annually, with a 10 % market increase in France every year from 1992 to 2004.[7] In L'Huissier's (2012) study of the slimming practices of working-class women in Northern France, use of topical firming creams featured as a physical technique employed by study participants (in addition to dietary regimes). The effectiveness of these kinds of creams, however, remains some matter of debate.

The language used to advertise these slimming creams uses a deliberately scientised register that could be due to the nature of the product: the brand may be keen to describe which ingredients facilitate skin-firming and what studies have been done to confirm this. On one level, the predominance of these products in the French market meant that more advertisements of this kind appeared in the data analysed. This could contribute towards an explanation of the French advertisements displaying more elements of scientised language. However, on a broader level, it could be suggested that if both French advertising copywriters and consumers are more accustomed to this type of register due to the popularity of these creams, then this discourse may influence or infiltrate other beauty product marketing in a French context.

These slimming creams, along with many other cosmetic products, are sold predominantly in pharmacies and 'parapharmacies' in France. The French 'parapharmacie' tends to sell non-prescription medicines and a range of skincare brands, and the staff—often wearing laboratory coats—are generally highly trained in the cosmetics products on offer and can offer a range of detailed advice. This advice does happen to a certain extent in UK, for example, on the beauty counters in Boots, but this tends to be given by different staff and in a physically different part of the shop to the pharmacy counter. The so-called 'French pharmacy brands' (such as *Vichy, Eucerin, La Roche Posay, Bioderma*, and many more) carry a certain prestige, perhaps over other European pharmacy brands. Not all of these products have previously been easily available outside of France, and there exist numerous blogs advising US and UK readers what to stock up on when they visit a French pharmacy, in addition to websites offering the chance to purchase French pharmacy brands to those living outside of France. These French pharmacy brands, perhaps quite predictably, tend to draw on scientised discourse that corresponds to the pharmacy and 'parapharmacie' contexts in which they are sold. A quick look at these sites, which contain detailed information and product reviews on French skincare, suggests there is a popular perception amongst UK and US consumers that the French pharmacy brands are superior and more effective than some of their British and American equivalents.

As explored in Chapter 3, the pattern of Problem-Solution discourse was found to be more frequent in the French advertisements than the British, and these differences were statistically significant. The Problem-Solution pattern may benefit from using a scientised register in order to emphasise exactly how a particular product can address skincare concerns (such as through a certain ingredient or formula), providing evidence and authenticity. In this context, it is perhaps not surprising that the French advertisements analysed displayed more of the Problem-Solution pattern and more of the scientised register than the British advertisements.

CONSUMER ATTITUDES

It is worth considering what effects these appeals to science might have on the target female consumer. Dodds et al. (2008) explored British consumer attitudes towards use of scientific claims in advertisements for 'functional foods' (such as probiotic yoghurts) and cosmetics. These two products are similar in that a 'scientific' register is used to persuade potential consumers of product benefits (Dodds et al. 2008: 211). They are also both 'experience' products in that product evaluation takes place after product purchase and usage (Dodds et al. 2008: 212). The study aimed to explore whether women found these claims believable, and they concluded that the consumer's scientific awareness affects how they interpret and critically assess advertising claims that draw on science (Dodds et al. 2008: 211–212). The participants in this particular study tended to be more incredulous, as opposed to confused, about the claims made in advertisements. In particular, they disliked the use of what they termed 'jargon' such as 'epidermal disorganization' and 'micro-cysts' (Dodds et al. 2008: 220). The focus groups for this study were relatively small, consisting of three focus groups each comprised of four to six female participants, as this was designed to be an exploratory investigation (Dodds et al. 2008: 215). The participants in this study had all worked in a scientific environment and had studied science to a certain level and were therefore likely to have a higher than average level of scientific awareness. This was a deliberate decision by the researchers: if the participants in the focus groups had difficulty making sense of the claims, then a member of the public with very little or no scientific background may struggle (Dodds et al. 2008: 213). However, their research concludes that consumers were sceptical and, at times, annoyed by this use of language.

GREEN BEAUTY: AN ALTERNATIVE DISCOURSE?

Seemingly running counter to this scientised register is the phenomenon of cosmetics brands marketing themselves as 'natural' or 'organic'. Often this discourse manifests itself through the suffix –free added to the lexical item: paraben-free, sulphate-free, alcohol-free, and so on, in addition to the emphasis on herbal and plant-based ingredients. 'No' lists are also common: no mineral oil, no perfume, and so on (Beerling 2014: 202). This trend is indicative of two recurrent themes in many contemporary Western societies: a growing concern over 'toxins' in cosmetics being potentially damaging to health, and a belief that natural is generally always preferable to synthetic or artificial. These ideas will be discussed more fully with reference to particular examples in the following paragraphs.

As with the scientised discourse, we encounter issues surrounding appropriate terminology. From the standpoint of the advertising regulatory bodies, there are some questions regarding certification of 'organic' and 'natural' products and what these claims really mean on product packaging. In most chemistry contexts, for example, 'organic' refers to compounds containing carbon; in beauty contexts it could mean anything from 'green', 'chemical free', or 'sold in organic shops', and the terms 'green' and 'chemical free' are not unproblematic (Romanowski 2011: 145–146). 'Organic' could mean that a certain percentage of the ingredients used are organic, and that this has been certified by organisations such as Cosmebio or the Soil Association, organisations that form part of the Cosmos Standard body, which ensures consistent labelling and product standards.[8] However, at present, brands are not obliged to join these bodies and some organic brands remain uncertified. The UK requirements for brand labelling are at the moment less stringent than those of France, which has set measurements for percentages of organic material in order for products to be labelled as such.[9] UK brands are encouraged to explain if the use of 'organic' on their labelling refers to a specific certification body, and the wording should not suggest that 'organic' has an understood meaning on cosmetics products.[10] It should be noted that these terms and their related lexis are often intended to provide connotations of a good product that is better for one's skin, hair, or body. Whether these products are indeed better for one's skin, hair, or body forms part of a wider debate, which is addressed later in this section.

As with the 'scientific' discourse, this 'natural' discourse has its own specialised vocabulary in order to emphasise product benefits. Examples of 'scientific/artificial ingredient' + **-free**, or **sans [without]** + 'scientific ingredient' are common:

Paraben-free (*Vichy* Liftactiv serum, *Elle* UK June 2011)

Sans paraben [**Paraben-free**] (*Mixa* Biovital Soin de Jour [day cream], *Elle* France 6 May 2011)

Sans colorant [**No colour**] (*BioSecûre* soins corporels [body care products], *Elle* France 3 June 2011)

Sans OGM [**No GM ingredients**] (*BioSecûre* soins corporels [body care products], *Elle* France 3 June 2011)

Ammonia-free (*L'Oréal* IONA professional permanent colour, *Elle* UK August 2011)

Sans matière issue de la pétrochimie [No petrochemically derived ingredients] (*BioSecūre* soins corporels [body care products], *Elle* France 3 June 2011)

Sans silicone, sans paraben [Silicone free, paraben free] (*Garnier* Fructis Pure Brilliance Shampooing et Après-shampooing [Pure Shine shampoo and conditioner], *Cosmopolitan* France June 2011)

The rhetorical effect of these discursive constructions is that the ingredient or item placed before *–free* or after *sans* is presumed to be undesirable and/or best avoided. By contrast, as this product is actively not including said ingredient, this could be a motive for purchase. This discourse could therefore be reminiscent of *sugar-free* and *fat-free* claims in food advertising, suggesting a healthier product. The French ARPP specifically addresses the phenomenon on 'Allégations 'sans'' [**'without' claims**], arguing that 'sans' should not be overused, as advertising should focus on what the product already *has*. In other words, positive discursive evaluations should be the main part of a given cosmetic advertisement: 'sans' claims should not form the basis of the advertisement, nor should they mislead the consumer as to the product formulation. This advice suggests that 'sans' or 'without' may be potentially confusing if consumers are led to believe the omission of a certain ingredient entails a safer product, which may not necessarily be the case.[11]

In addition to the absence of various 'artificial' ingredients, certain 'natural' ingredients tend to be emphasised in more 'natural' beauty advertisements. For example:

Turmeric (*Clarins* Daily Energizers skincare, *Elle* UK September 2011)

Alchemilla (*Clarins* Daily Energizers skincare, *Elle* UK September 2011)

Argan oil (*VO5* Miracle Concentrate hair treatment, *Cosmopolitan* UK September 2011)

Gingko biloba (*Clarins* Daily Energizers skincare, *Elle* UK September 2011)

La mangue [mango] (*Klorane* masque au beurre de mangue [mango butter hair masque], *Cosmopolitan* France August 2011)

Rhamnose (*Vichy* Liftactiv Derm Source skincare, *Elle* UK June 2011)

Natural oils (*E45* Endless Moisture Derma-Restore body lotion, *Elle* UK June 2011)

Mango and shea butters (*Clinique* Chubby Stick lip tint, *Cosmopolitan* July UK 2011)

These ingredients are presumed to be positive, although in some cases they are perhaps unfamiliar to most consumers and, like the scientific ingredients, merit an explanation later in the advertising text. This emphasis on natural ingredients over synthetic ones can be viewed as a growing belief of many citizens in Western societies that natural is good; synthetic/artificial is bad (Romanowski 2011: 165; Romanowski and Schueller 2013: 224–225). These notions are particularly prevalent in the fields of food, cosmetics, household products, and childbirth. Of course, natural is not always better: manufactured ingredients may be subject to safer lab testing; some of the deadliest poisons are 'natural'; and there is not always an agreed-upon definition of what 'natural' is (Romanowski 2011: 165). Avoiding some synthetic ingredients may be better for some people who cannot tolerate them, but natural alternatives are not without issues (as people who have severe skin reactions to aloe vera and essential oils can attest). As with the scientised discourse, trying to find out whether products actually are 'natural' and which ingredients should be avoided is a real challenge. There is an enormous wealth of information from environmental groups,[12] concerned consumers and charities, and organic cosmetics companies, in addition to a range of books[13] providing 'toxicity' lists linking some cosmetics to serious diseases, including cancer. There are even mobile phone apps that you can use to scan cosmetic barcodes, identify potentially dangerous ingredients, and choose your skincare purchases accordingly.[14] In the USA, this movement has gained a lot of momentum and media attention, with groups and individuals lobbying various companies and even the government. On the other hand, cosmetics companies, industry experts, and government bodies tend to stress that the levels of these ingredients are much too low to have any adverse effect. Some cosmetics scientists and scientific bodies take issue with many of the misrepresentations of cosmetics science research in the media, arguing that most of the debate is in fact sensationalist scare-mongering.[15] Many industry experts tend to suggest there is little peer-reviewed evidence behind much of the furore, but the potential negative effects of long-term use of chemicals is something that might need to be explored through further, in-depth research (Beerling 2014: 202).

Within this debate, one category of ingredient which has attracted a lot of attention is that of parabens, as we have seen in the emphasis on **paraben-free** in some earlier advertisement examples. Concerns over paraben safety have been escalating since the study by Darbe et al. (2004) that found parabens in human breast tumours—although it is not clear what, if any, connection there is to parabens in cosmetics, and further research needs to be done (Romanowski 2011: 160). Parabens preserve cosmetics and protect against microbial growth, and so appropriate alternatives need to be carefully and seriously considered (Romanowski 2011: 160). The US FDA states that at present there is no reason to be concerned about parabens in personal care products at current levels.[16] The EU, however, has been more precautionary in its approach and has recently banned a number of parabens,[17] widening the gap between what ingredients are allowed in EU versus US cosmetic products (Beerling 2014: 202). This may have implications on product formulas, with satisfactory alternatives needed.[18]

WITH PEPTIDES OR PARABEN-FREE?

It should be emphasised that the majority of product advertisements are not necessarily being dishonest on their advertising copy, but that the representations of 'science' and 'nature' may potentially be misleading in certain contexts. As the cosmetics market continues to increase, brands are faced with quite complex decisions surrounding demands for ever-more effective product formulas and concerns over 'toxic overload' and ingredient safety. The wealth of information online surrounding which chemicals should be avoided in cosmetics is, at times, confusing and contradictory. Cosmetics advertisements that focus on the 'science' and those that focus on the 'natural' often have their own different vocabularies, which are not always transparent.

Perhaps most interesting, the 'scientific' and the 'natural' discourses seem to be becoming increasingly combined by brands; for example, '10X more concentrated in [natural ingredient]'. In some cases, this may be entirely legitimate. For example, French pharmacy brand *Avène* has its own hydrotherapy medical centre: patients can be referred for a stay here by their dermatologist as the brand's water has been shown to have healing properties for burns, dermatitis, and other skin conditions. In cases like this, it is probably an obvious choice for the brand to emphasise the connections between 'science' and 'nature'. However, there is not always such a clear-cut dichotomy: this does not mean to say that even if a brand has legitimate reason to appeal to both nature and science that its advertising materials could never be misleading. A related and complicating factor that we can add to the debate is a phenomenon increasingly known as *greenwashing*, in which cosmetics companies attempt to make their product appear more 'natural' or environmentally friendly than it really is. There is an ever-growing number of internet resources exposing brands that may not be as entirely 'natural' as their advertising discourse suggests. This is, again, indicative of the growing demand for accessible and transparent consumer information. The analysis of the discourse of 'nature' and 'science' in this chapter has aimed to demonstrate that the choices of 'with peptides' or 'paraben-free' are not so diametrically opposed as perhaps first imagined.

NOTES

1. The US Food and Drug Administration offers this definition; see http://www.fda.gov/Cosmetics/Labeling/Claims/ucm127064.htm
2. More AHA information available at http://www.fda.gov/Cosmetics/ProductsIngredients/Ingredients/ucm107940.htm
3. See for example a popular blog by a group of cosmetics scientists at http://www.thebeautybrains.com; so-called 'Cosmetics Cop' Paula Begoun's advice book (2012) and online ingredient dictionary at http://www.paulaschoice.com; and Ben Goldacre's blog at http://www.badscience.net, in which he addresses a range of issues connected to the popular (mis)representation of science.
4. See http://www.eucerin.co.uk/about-eucerin/philosophy
5. See http://www.vichy.co.uk/articles/ideal-skin-diagnosis/a21677.aspx and http://www.vichy.fr/article/diagnostic-peau-ideale/a20864.aspx

6. See http://www.clinique.co.uk/diagnostics and http://www.fr.clinique. com/diagnostics
7. Figures from http://www.dailymail.co.uk/health/article-261304/A-slimming-cream-works.html; unfortunately the article provided no follow-up references to verify these, but these figures can be found in similar news reports.
8. See http://www.cosmebio.org; http://www.soilassociation.org; and http://www.cosmos-standard.org
9. Most recent French guidelines are available here: http://www.arpp-pub. org/IMG/pdf/Produits_Cosmetiques-2.pdf
10. This is the advice given by the Committee of Advertising Practice on how best to comply with the ASA guidelines: https://www.cap.org.uk/Advice-Training-on-the-rules/Advice-Online-Database/Organic-General.aspx#. Vt7ClfmLTIU
11. These are part of the guidelines given here: http://www.arpp-pub.org/ IMG/pdf/Produits_Cosmetiques-2.pdf
12. One notable group is the Campaign for Safe Cosmetics: http://www.safe-cosmetics.org/
13. See for example Mellowship (2009), Deacon (2011), and Padgett (2015).
14. Think Dirty® Shop Clean is one of the most well-known of these kinds of apps: http://www.thinkdirtyapp.com
15. Romanowski and Schueller (2013) aim to explain some of these issues. See also relevant information on http://www.senseaboutscience.org/
16. See their full statement at http://www.fda.gov/Cosmetics/Products Ingredients/Ingredients/ucm128042.htm
17. More information here: http://europa.eu/rapid/press-release_IP-14-1051_en.htm
18. Another issue related to 'natural' products is that previously they have tended to be much more expensive than conventional products, as well as being less effective (for example, body wash may not lather sufficiently and therefore much more product is required) (Romanowski 2011: 146). This is now starting to change, with consumers demanding better quality products (Sheehan 2014: 289).

REFERENCES

Beerling, J. (2014). Green formulations and ingredients. In A. Sahota (Ed.), *Sustainability: How the cosmetics industry is greening up* (pp. 197–216). Chichester: Wiley.
Begoun, P. (2012). *Don't go to the cosmetics counter without me* (9th ed.). Washington: Beginning Press.

Chaiken, S. (1987). The heuristic model of persuasion. In M. Zanna, J. Olson, & C. Herman (Eds.), *Social influence: The Ontario Symposium* (Vol. 5, pp. 3–39). Hillsdale: Lawrence Erlbaum.

Coupland, J. (2003). Ageist ideology and discourses of control in skincare product marketing. In J. Coupland & R. Gwyn (Eds.), *Discourse, the body and identity* (pp. 127–150). Basingstoke: Palgrave Macmillan.

Coupland, J. (2007). Gendered discourses on the 'problem' of ageing: Consumerised solutions. *Discourse and Communication, 1*(1), 37–61.

Darbe, P., Aljarrah, A., Miller, W., Goldham, N., Saver, M., & Pope, G. (2004). Concentrations of parabens in human breast tumours. *Toxicology, 24*(1), 5–13.

Davies, M. (2008). *The corpus of contemporary English: 520 million words, 1990 – Present*. Available online at http://corpus.byu.edu/coca/.

Deacon, G. (2011). *There's lead in your lipstick*. Toronto: Penguin Group (Canada).

Dodds, R., Tseelon, E., & Weitkamp, E. (2008). Making sense of scientific claims in advertising: A study of scientifically aware consumers. *Public Understanding of Science, 17*(2), 211–230.

Fairclough, N. (1992). *Discourse and social change*. Cambridge: Polity Press.

Goldacre, B. (2009). *Bad science*. London: Harper Perennial.

Harrison, C. (2008). Real men do wear mascara: Advertising discourse and masculine identity. *Critical Discourse Studies, 5*(1), 55–73.

Harrison, C. (2012). Studio5ive.com: Selling cosmetics to men and reconstructing masculine identity. In K. Ross (Ed.), *The handbook of gender, sex and media* (pp. 189–204). London: Wiley-Blackwell.

Jeffries, L. (2007). *The textual construction of the female body: A critical discourse analysis approach*. Basingstoke: Palgrave Macmillan.

Kress, G., & van Leeuwen, T. (2006). *Reading images: The grammar of visual design* (2nd ed.). London: Routledge.

L'Huissier, A. (2012). The weight-loss practices of working class women in France. *Food, Culture and Society: An International Journal of Multidisciplinary Research, 15*(4), 643–664.

Mellowship, D. (2009). *Toxic beauty: How hidden chemicals in cosmetics harm you*. London: Gaia.

Padgett, P. (2015). *The green beauty rules: The essential guide to toxic-free beauty, green glamour, and glowing skin*. Deerfield Beach: Health Communications, Inc.

Ringrow, H. (2014) 'Peptides, proteins and peeling active ingredients: exploring 'scientific' language in English and French cosmetics advertising'. *Études de Stylistique Anglaise*, no. 7, pp. 183–210.

Romanowski, P., & Creators of Thebeautybrains.com. (2011). *Can you get hooked on lip balm?: Top cosmetic scientists answer your questions about the lotions, potions and other beauty products you use every day*. Ontario: Harlequin.

Romanowski, P., & Schueller, R. (2013). *It's OK to have lead in your lipstick*. US: Brains Publishing.

Sheehan, K. (2014). Targeting the green consumer. In A. Sahota (Ed.), *Sustainability: How the cosmetics industry is greening up* (pp. 289–300). Chichester: Wiley.

Tungate, M. (2011). *Branded beauty: How marketing changed the way we look*. London: Kogan Page.

CHAPTER 6

The Case for Feminist Critical Discourse Analysis

Abstract This final chapter reflects upon the approach employed in this book, which is Feminist Critical Discourse Analysis (Lazar 2005a, 2007). This framework, which has not been universally adopted amongst language and gender scholars, critically analyses texts from a feminist perspective and can be viewed as a sub-discipline of Critical Discourse Analysis. This chapter explores how the key principles of Feminist Critical Discourse Analysis are used in this book, and finishes by examining the role of this paradigm in challenging media assumptions.

Keywords Feminist Critical Discourse Analysis • Critical Discourse Analysis • Language and gender • Media representations

FEMINIST CRITICAL DISCOURSE ANALYSIS: THEORY AND PRACTICE

The approach that has been used in this book falls under the remit of Feminist Critical Discourse Analysis (FCDA), a paradigm which can be attributed to Lazar (2005a, 2007). This framework was introduced in Chapter 1, where it was suggested that FCDA critically analyses texts from a feminist perspective (Lazar 2005a, 2007). FCDA can perhaps

© The Editor(s) (if applicable) and The Author(s) 2016
H. Ringrow, *The Language of Cosmetics Advertising*,
DOI 10.1057/978-1-137-55798-8_6

most productively be viewed as sub-discipline of Critical Discourse Analysis (CDA) as a whole. As mentioned earlier, *critical* denotes a denaturalising strategy: it points to an analysis beyond description of detailed linguistic features, moving towards an examination of *how* and *why* these features may be used to serve certain ideological purposes in social contexts (Fairclough 2010: 10–11; Machin and Mayr 2012: 4). In doing so, CDA can be seen as normative in that it '[…] addresses social wrongs in their discursive aspects and possible ways of righting or mitigating them' (Fairclough 2010: 11). CDA is therefore often viewed as both theory *and* method because (a) it argues that ideology is encoded in language and (b) it provides a framework for language analysis, often from a particular socio-political viewpoint. Theoretically speaking, CDA generally holds a Hallidayan approach to language. In broad terms, it takes as a starting point for most research that language structure makes particular meanings in everyday life (Bloor and Bloor 2004: 2). Consequently, the tools of Systemic Functional Linguistics are sometimes used as part of CDA's research methodologies (Eggins 2004: 11).

CDA has of course not been without its critiques, often from a methodological standpoint.[1] Some of the main shortcomings that have been identified include a failure to adequately engage with quantitative methodologies, where appropriate; a suggestion that CDA's linguistic analysis is ad-hoc and impressionistic; and concerns that texts chosen for analysis are often selected to fit in with one's preconceived ideas. A number of scholars have challenged and addressed these criticisms in recent publications. For example, CDA has of late been making more use of corpus linguistic techniques in addition to ensuring transparent and replicable qualitative and quantitative linguistic analysis (Machin and Mayr 2012: 214–215; for examples of this in action see Baker 2006, 2009, 2010, 2014; Baker and Levon 2015). These techniques can help to further improve CDA research, which, despite its potential shortcomings, I believe provides an appropriate paradigm for research that explores language in its social context. It is also important to emphasise that CDA has never attempted to provide a unified theory or methodology, which inevitably leads to much variation in its research. As such, critiques should be specific to the type of CDA research which is being applied (Weiss and Wodak 2008: 12–13).

Gender and language research can often be best situated within a CDA approach. CDA has been used '[…] most extensively by feminist linguists to produce critical examinations of representations of gender through media discourses' as it can provide an appropriate linguistic framework to carry out some of the aims and objectives of feminist linguistics (Mills and Mullany 2011: 78).

Arguably, some might question why there is the need for an explicit feminist label, since CDA as a whole tends to be concerned with social injustice as represented and reinforced in language and imagery, and the discursive construction of gender falls within this remit (Lazar 2005b: 2). However, the grouping together of FCDA scholarship under this relatively new term may be a productive development that opens up the possibility for shared interests and collaborations between feminist scholars across national boundaries, with the additional aim of raising the profile of gender research in CDA (Lazar 2005b: 3–4). Wodak (2008) suggests that FCDA presupposes a focus on gender as opposed to other relevant variables, and has called for a consideration of multiple contextual factors in FCDA research, where appropriate.[2]

Feminist CDA research has tended to be found across a range of journals and edited volumes but has not yet made itself known as a cohesive body of research (Lazar 2005b: 34). FCDA can be viewed as interdisciplinary as it contributes a feminist perspective to Critical Discourse Studies in addition to suggesting the relevance of language to feminist research (Lazar 2007: 142). Lazar outlines the main goal of FCDA as: '[…] to show up the complex, subtle, and sometimes not so subtle, ways in which frequently taken-for-granted gendered assumptions and hegemonic power relations are discursively produced, sustained, negotiated, and challenged in different contexts and communities' (2007: 142). A connection is therefore made between what 'gets done' though discourse and how this has real-life consequences, in terms of female (and male) media representation. Advertising is a key site for exploring gendered relations within FCDA because of the ubiquity of advertisements in the public sphere (Lazar 2007: 156, 160). For the purposes of this project, FCDA provided a framework from which to examine the 'gendered discourse' (Sunderland 2004) of cosmetics advertising in a cross-cultural perspective, investigating how women are addressed and represented through the French and English beauty advertisements analysed. As suggested throughout the book, the tools used for analysis were flexible in response to the data, which is the case in much CDA, and FCDA, research.

KEY PRINCIPLES OF FCDA IN ACTION

Lazar (2005b: 5–19, 2007: 145–155) identifies what she regards as the five key tenets of FCDA research. In this book, I have endeavoured to show these principles in action. The first is that of feminist analytical resistance, that is, making sense of how social practices are discursively constructed can be viewed as a first step in furthering the cause of gender equality. In doing so, feminist linguists hold a non-neutral stance, in that they believe that their work should be a useful catalyst, alongside a range of other feminist activism, for progress in gender equality. It is my hope that this book has contributed in some small way to this cause, in terms of identifying the gendered assumptions in contemporary cosmetics advertising discourse.

The second principle of FCDA involves conceptualising gender as an ideological construct that is often used to uphold existing ideas and/or power relations. Through the analysis in this book, I have argued that the model of femininity identified in current cosmetics advertising can be framed within the construct of Consumer/Commodified Femininity (Talbot 2010b; Benwell and Stokoe 2006). This connection between purchasing beauty products and achieving a desirable female appearance is a construction that fits neatly within a neo-liberal consumerist context and serves to reinforce gender differences. This was examined in particular in Chapter 3 through the adaptation and application of Hoey's (1983, 2001) Problem-Solution pattern to beauty advertisements. Cosmetic 'solutions' were provided to the 'problems' of female appearance, a stressful lifestyle and environment, and existing cosmetics which apparently under-perform. Chapter 4 explored the connections made between femininity and sensuality, both in terms of idealising the sensualised female body and the emphasis on the sensory, pleasurable experience of using beauty products. Chapter 5 focused on the scientised discourse of current cosmetics advertising, discussing a range of strategies that are employed in order to increase a sense of authenticity and link these products to overall health and well-being.

The third tenet of FCDA is the acknowledgement that gender and power relations in current society tend to be complex, and feminist analyses have contributed and hopefully will continue to contribute to a better understanding of this complexity. Social media technologies provide a platform for the contemporary consumer to discuss some of the problems (and, although admittedly less frequently, the positives) associated with many cosmetics advertising campaigns. This can most clearly be seen in the response to the marketing strategies of the beauty brand *Dove*, which has attracted a huge amount of popular attention in both mainstream and alternative media, blogs, and (of course) in the world of the YouTube comments sections. Some of the debates have centred around the use of 'real' models in their campaigns; the company's charity endeavours in terms of eating disorder support networks; the continual emphasis made between appearance and self-worth in their advertisements; and how *Dove*'s brand ethos fits within its parent company Unilever, who also owns *Axe/Lynx* (arguably, a brand not known for its progressive gender representations).[3] Increased critical media literacy teaching in schools may also be helpful in terms of teaching young people strategies for exploring and challenging media representations, although there are debates surrounding why, how, and when this should be taught.[4] As discussed in Chapter 1, female consumers may have a range of thoughts and feelings about cosmetics advertising and even cosmetics themselves, and are influenced by different factors. In addition to exploring opinions through social media forums, Reader Response analysis in terms of focus groups where women examine and discuss advertisements would be a potential future research area that could explore real women's reactions to cosmetics advertising language. Ideally, this research would involve both Metropolitan French and British English readers, to reflect the data analysed in this book. Reader Response studies can offer an important and complementary perspective to critical linguistic analysis. A rigorous textual analysis, which is arguably beneficial in itself in order to deconstruct the language used, can usually only ever *suggest* how people may react to media discourse (Benwell and Stokoe 2006: 166; Gauntlett 2008: 167). In this context, it is often productive to consider overall group views on advertising as well as individual opinions, which may be extremely complex and at times contradictory (Gauntlett 2008: 278–289).[5]

The fourth principle of FCDA holds that discourse is key in the (de)construction of gender, in terms of how gendered norms are reproduced and negotiated in text and talk in different contexts. FCDA can therefore be used to analyse contextualised examples of discourse. In the data explored in this book, the overall societal and media contexts have been considered in addition to the different linguistic and cultural contexts of Metropolitan France and the UK. Overall, the French advertisements contained more statistically significant occurrences of Problem-Solution patterns (Chapter 3), nudity (Chapter 4), and 'scientised' discourse (Chapter 5). The prevalence of Problem-Solution discourse in the French data could be linked to the tendency for the French advertisements to use more scientised language, which might be more likely to emphasise 'problems' or 'solutions' related to a medico-scientific register, especially in the advertising of the French slimming creams. The increased number of advertisements featuring some form of nudity in the French data may correspond to a generally more relaxed attitude to nudity in French media culture, supporting the findings of Biswas et al. (1992), who found that there were more visual sexual appeals in French advertising than in that of the UK. However, a further complicating factor in the analysis of the nudity is that sometimes it is arguably not used in a primarily sensual manner, but to connect the body (or, more accurately, the particular body part) to a 'scientific' solution. In some examples, the use of nudity may be two-fold: to increase the sensuality and to highlight the physical body part that is targeted by the product being advertised. In practice, it is sometimes difficult to ascertain which usage is foregrounded. Besides nudity, overall sensual discourse displayed comparable frequencies of occurrence in the English and the French data, and any differences were not statistically significant. This finding could suggest that sensual discourse is employed to a similar extent in both French and English cosmetics advertising contexts, but that the English sensual discourse may contain other elements in lieu of the increased nudity in the French data. Further research could explore these subtle distinctions in more detail.

Finally, inherent to FCDA is critical reflexivity as praxis, which encompasses broader reflections on the construction of gender and self-reflexivity for researchers, in order to achieve the ultimate goal of social progress and transformation. As such, '[…] a discursive critique of the prevailing limiting structures is a step in that direction' (Lazar 2005b: 15–16). The conclusions drawn in this book, although they may have wider implications, can, as always, only be confidently applied to the data analysed. The analysis was also limited mainly to the textual domain due to the difficulty in image reproduction, as explained in the introductory chapter. In reflecting upon the constructions of femininity discussed in the book, the discourses of 'empowerment', 'choice', and 'egalitarianism' in a form of Commodity Feminism (Goldman 1992) should be of particular interest to FCDA. This is not just a case of advertisers appropriating feminism for profit, but it may potentially devalue some of the key tenets of feminism itself (Lazar 2007: 151–153). Lazar also calls for continual reflexivity of feminist scholars' own theoretical positions and practices in order to ensure the progress of feminist activism in its different forms (2007: 152).

THE ROLE OF FCDA IN CHALLENGING MEDIA ASSUMPTIONS: FUTURE DIRECTIONS

This book has explored how femininity is discursively constructed in contemporary British English and Metropolitan French media contexts. The approach of FCDA has been used to unpack and challenge axiomatic gendered assumptions in beauty advertising. It has intended to show that these constructions of femininity are not necessarily global self-evident truths but have been created and/or reinforced through media discourses. The portrayal of ageing as something that needs immediate disguising through a cosmetic solution (Chapter 3); the use of semi-clothed women to appeal to a predominantly heterosexual demographic (Chapter 4); the need for lipstick to have a hi-tech 'scientific formula' (Chapter 5): all of these notions are not inherently natural, but may have become *naturalised* as part of the discourse of everyday life. As emphasised throughout this book, the reader may instinctively be sceptical of advertising claims and language.

This analysis, then, is intended to help shed light on *why* she may feel this way. The representation of the female body in the advertisements analysed is generally presented as in need of fixing. In this sphere, women are never appreciated, to paraphrase from *Bridget Jones's Diary*, just the way they are. Looking 'good' is almost always associated with modes of consumption, leaving little space for attractiveness outside of this realm. The various appeals to 'science' may simultaneously patronise and confuse women by presenting a diluted stereotype of what science actually is while using undecipherable language (Goldacre 2009: 26–27). Even for the critical consumer (and arguably this type of consumer may now be the norm), these media constructs are incredibly pervasive and finding counter-truths can sometimes be difficult to articulate and disseminate effectively (Jeffries 2007: 194–199; Harrison 2012: 201). The more aware we are of the intricacies of female media representations, the more we can do to challenge them with alternatives from women's own lives, non-mainstream media sources, or both. These challenges should not be underestimated: they may involve substantial cultural shifts in addition to changing one's cognitive and conceptual frameworks, such as not viewing ageing appearance as undesirable (Coupland 2003: 147–148). As such, this book has not intended to argue that all cosmetics advertisements are deceptive or misleading. This is not the case. Rather, it has aimed at exploring some of the underlying assumptions found in beauty marketing discourse. It has also aimed at expanding the tools we have available to analyse cosmetics advertising as a sub-genre of advertising. For women who want to make informed decisions about what products they put on their faces and bodies, exploring the claims in advertisements may give them more information to make their choices. One of these choices, of course, should include opting out. Wolf (1991: 273) suggests that '[...] the problem with cosmetics exists only when women feel invisible or inadequate without them', and arguably this problem is often not helped by the marketing techniques of the cosmetics industry.

Critical linguistic research into beauty advertising and related areas can be seen as an important first step in challenging the status quo. Ultimately, feminist scholars are working towards achieving the goals of equality and social justice for both men and women (Lazar 2007: 153; 160 Baker 2008: 263). The rise of the male cosmetics market and beauty advertising to men raises some interesting questions in this regard, as men are now being increasingly encouraged to turn their gaze to their own 'problematic' body parts (Harrison 2008, 2012). We must continue to envisage and work towards an alternative landscape in which everyone, regardless of gender identity and sexual orientation, can have real freedom of choice in all domains.

NOTES

1. See for example Toolan (1997) and Poole (2010) for overviews of key critiques of CDA.
2. Wodak (2008) also interviews groups of migrant women using a methodology that combines FCDA and CDA: Discourse-Historical approaches.
3. See for example Banet-Weiser (2012: 42–43).
4. Scholars within childhood education have raised questions around the idea of teaching children media literacy skills, including what critical literacy actually is and how and why it should be taught, and some argue that critical media training is not always appropriate and/or useful within formal education settings (see discussions in Buckingham 2003, 2007, 2011; Livingstone 2002, 2009).
5. Reader Response to cosmetics is further complicated in that it can be difficult to ascertain exact correlations between cosmetics advertising and actual product purchasing.

REFERENCES

Baker, P. (2006). *Using corpora in discourse analysis*. London: Continuum.
Baker, P. (2008). *Sexed texts: Language, gender and sexuality*. London: Equinox.
Baker, P. (2009). *Contemporary corpus linguistics*. London: Continuum.
Baker, P. (2010). *Sociolinguistics and corpus linguistics*. Edinburgh: Edinburgh University Press.
Baker, P. (2014). *Using corpora to analyse gender*. London: Bloomsbury.
Baker, P., & Levon, E. (2015). Picking the right cherries?: A comparison of corpus-based and qualitative analyses of news articles about masculinity. *Discourse and Communication, 9*(2), 221–336.
Banet-Weiser, S. (2012). *Authentic™: The politics of ambivalence in a brand culture*. New York: New York University Press.
Benwell, B., & Stokoe, E. (2006). *Discourse and identity*. Edinburgh: Edinburgh University Press.

Biswas, A., Olsen, J., & Carlet, V. (1992). A comparison of print advertisements from the United States and France. *Journal of Advertising, 21*(4), 73–81.

Bloor, M., & Bloor, T. (2004). *The functional analysis of English* (2nd ed.). London: Hodder Arnold.

Buckingham, D. (2003). *Media education: Literacy, learning and contemporary culture.* Cambridge: Polity Press.

Buckingham, D. (2007). *Beyond technology: Children's learning in the age of digital media.* Cambridge: Polity Press.

Buckingham, D. (2011). *The material child: Growing up in consumer culture.* Cambridge: Polity Press.

Coupland, J. (2003). Ageist ideology and discourses of control in skincare product marketing. In J. Coupland & R. Gwyn (Eds.), *Discourse, the body and identity* (pp. 127–150). Basingstoke: Palgrave Macmillan.

Eggins, S. (2004). *An introduction to systemic functional linguistics* (2nd ed.). London: Routledge.

Fairclough, N. (2010). *Critical discourse analysis: The critical study of language* (2nd ed.). London: Routledge.

Gauntlett, D. (2008). *Media, gender and identity: An introduction* (2nd ed.). London: Routledge.

Goldacre, B. (2009). *Bad science.* London: Harper Perennial.

Goldman, R. (1992). *Reading ads socially.* London/New York: Routledge.

Harrison, C. (2008). Real men do wear mascara: Advertising discourse and masculine identity. *Critical Discourse Studies, 5*(1), 55–73.

Harrison, C. (2012). Studio5ive.com: Selling cosmetics to men and reconstructing masculine identity. In K. Ross (Ed.), *The handbook of gender, sex and media* (pp. 189–204). London: Wiley-Blackwell.

Hoey, M. (1983). *On the surface of discourse.* London: Allen and Unwin.

Hoey, M. (2001). *Textual interaction: An introduction to written discourse analysis.* London: Routledge.

Jeffries, L. (2007). *The textual construction of the female body: A critical discourse analysis approach.* Basingstoke: Palgrave Macmillan.

Lazar, M. (Ed.). (2005a). *Feminist critical discourse analysis: Gender, power and ideology in discourse.* Basingstoke: Palgrave Macmillan.

Lazar, M. (2005b). Politicising gender in discourse: Feminist critical discourse analysis as political perspective and praxis. In M. Lazar (Ed.), *Feminist critical discourse analysis: Gender, power and ideology in discourse* (pp. 1–30). Basingstoke: Palgrave Macmillan.

Lazar, M. (2007). Feminist critical discourse analysis: Articulating a feminist discourse praxis. *Critical Discourse Studies, 1*(2), 141–164.

Livingstone, S. (2002). *Young people and new media: Childhood and the changing media environment.* London: SAGE.

Livingstone, S. (2009). *Children and the Internet: Great expectations, challenging realities.* London: Polity Press.

Machin, D., & Mayr, A. (2012). *How to do critical discourse analysis: A multimodal introduction*. London: SAGE.

Mills, S., & Mullany, L. (2011). *Language, gender and feminism: Theory, methodology and practice*. London: Routledge.

Poole, B. (2010). Commitment and criticality: Fairclough's critical discourse analysis evaluated. *International Journal of Applied Linguistics, 2*(1), 137–155.

Sunderland, J. (2004). *Gendered discourses*. Basingstoke: Palgrave Macmillan.

Talbot, M. (2010). *Language, intertextuality and subjectivity: Voices in the construction of consumer femininity*. Saarbrücken: Lambert Academic Publishing.

Toolan, M. (1997). What is critical discourse analysis and why are people saying such terrible things about it? *Language and Literature, 6*(2), 83–103.

Weiss, G., & Wodak, R. (2008). Theory, interdisciplinarity and critical discourse analysis. In G. Weiss & R. Wodak (Eds.), *Critical discourse analysis: Theory and interdisciplinarity* (pp. 1–34). Basingstoke: Palgrave Macmillan.

Wodak, R. (2008). Controversial issues in feminist critical discourse analysis. In K. Harrington, L. Litosseliti, H. Sauntson, & J. Sunderland (Eds.), *Gender and language research methodologies* (pp. 193–210). Basingstoke: Palgrave Macmillan.

Wolf, N. (1991). *The beauty myth: How images of beauty are used against women*. London: Vintage.

Index

© The Editor(s) (if applicable) and The Author(s) 2016   115
H. Ringrow, *The Language of Cosmetics Advertising*,
DOI 10.1057/978-1-137-55798-8

Printed by Printforce, the Netherlands